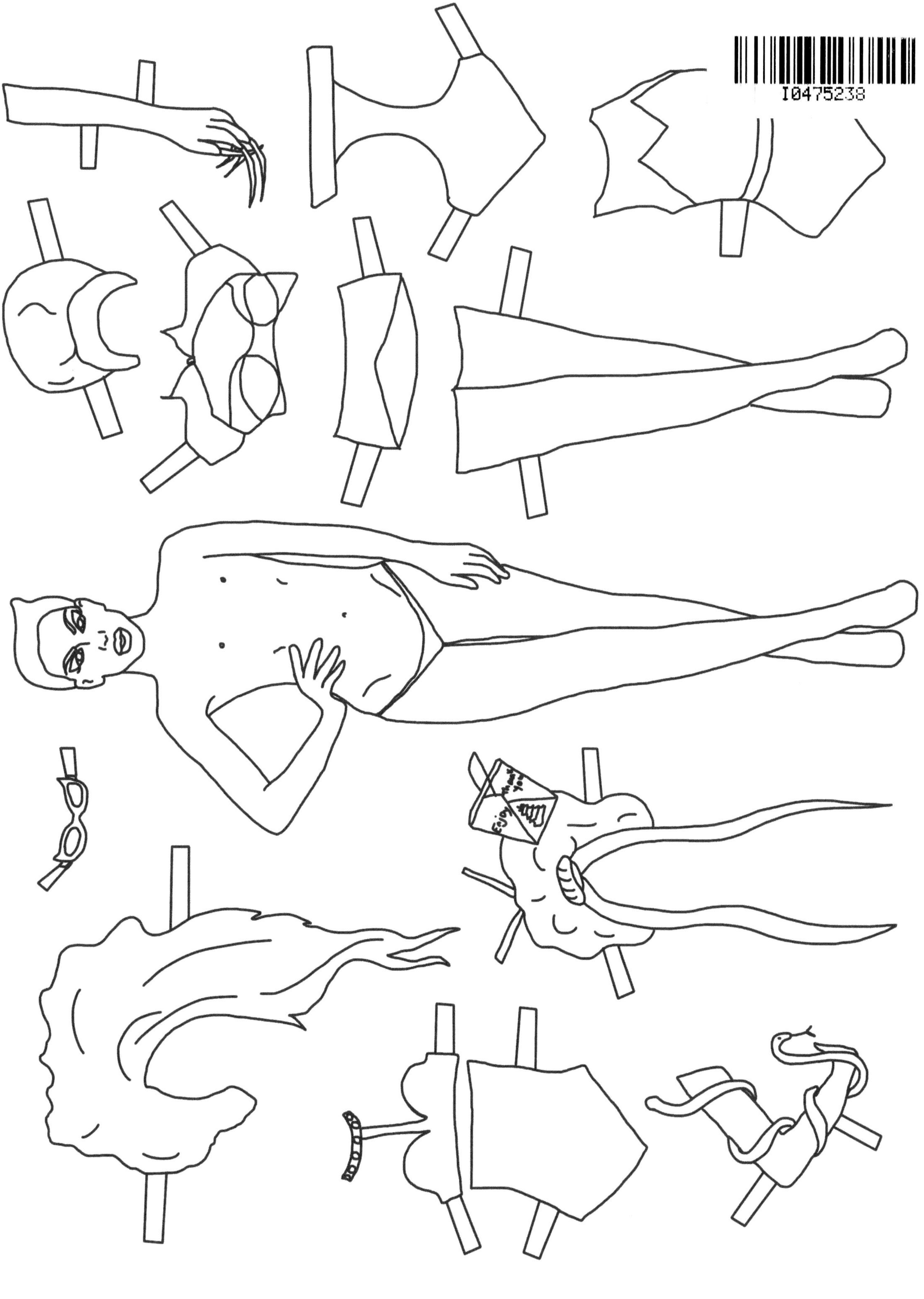

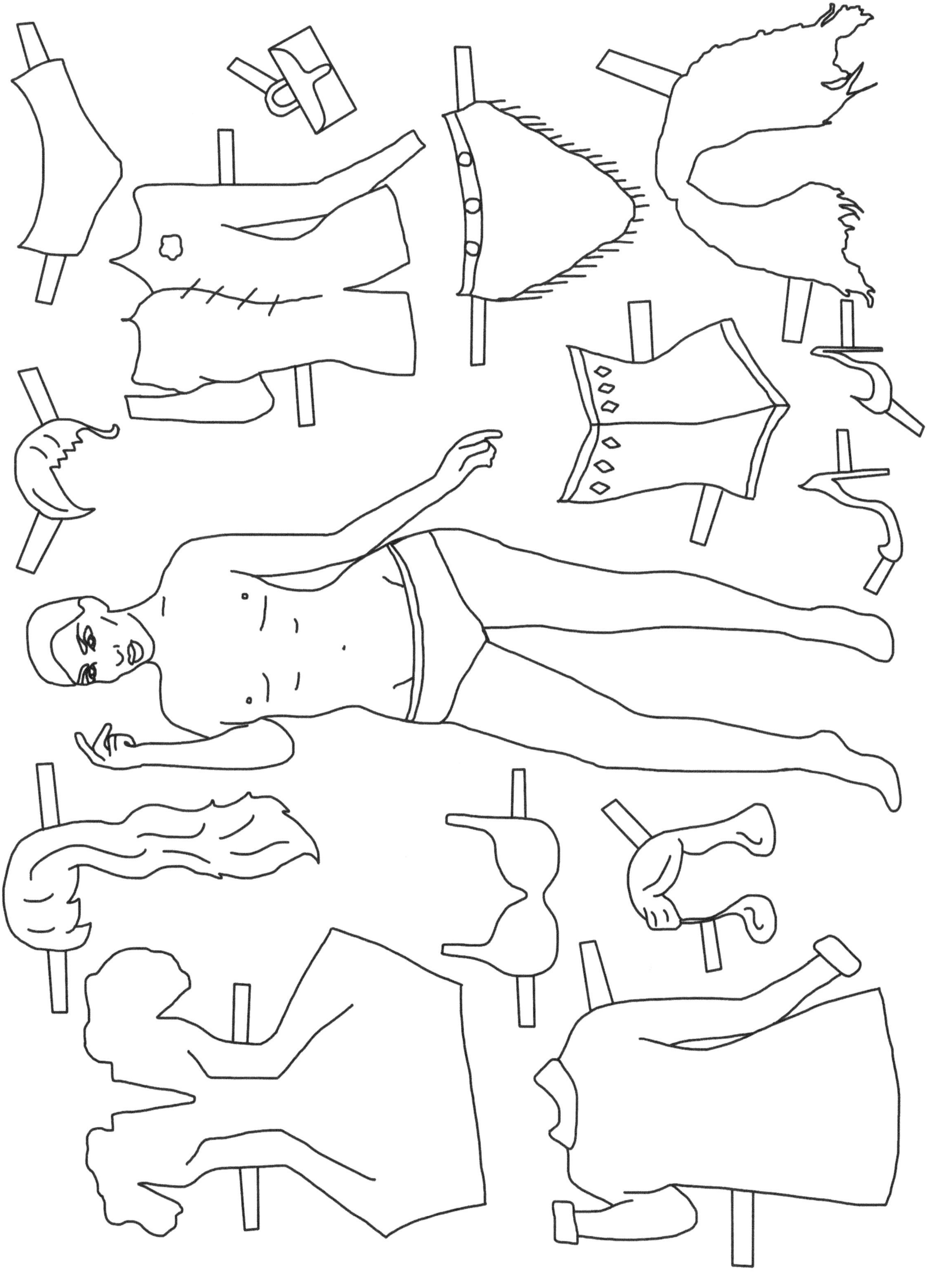

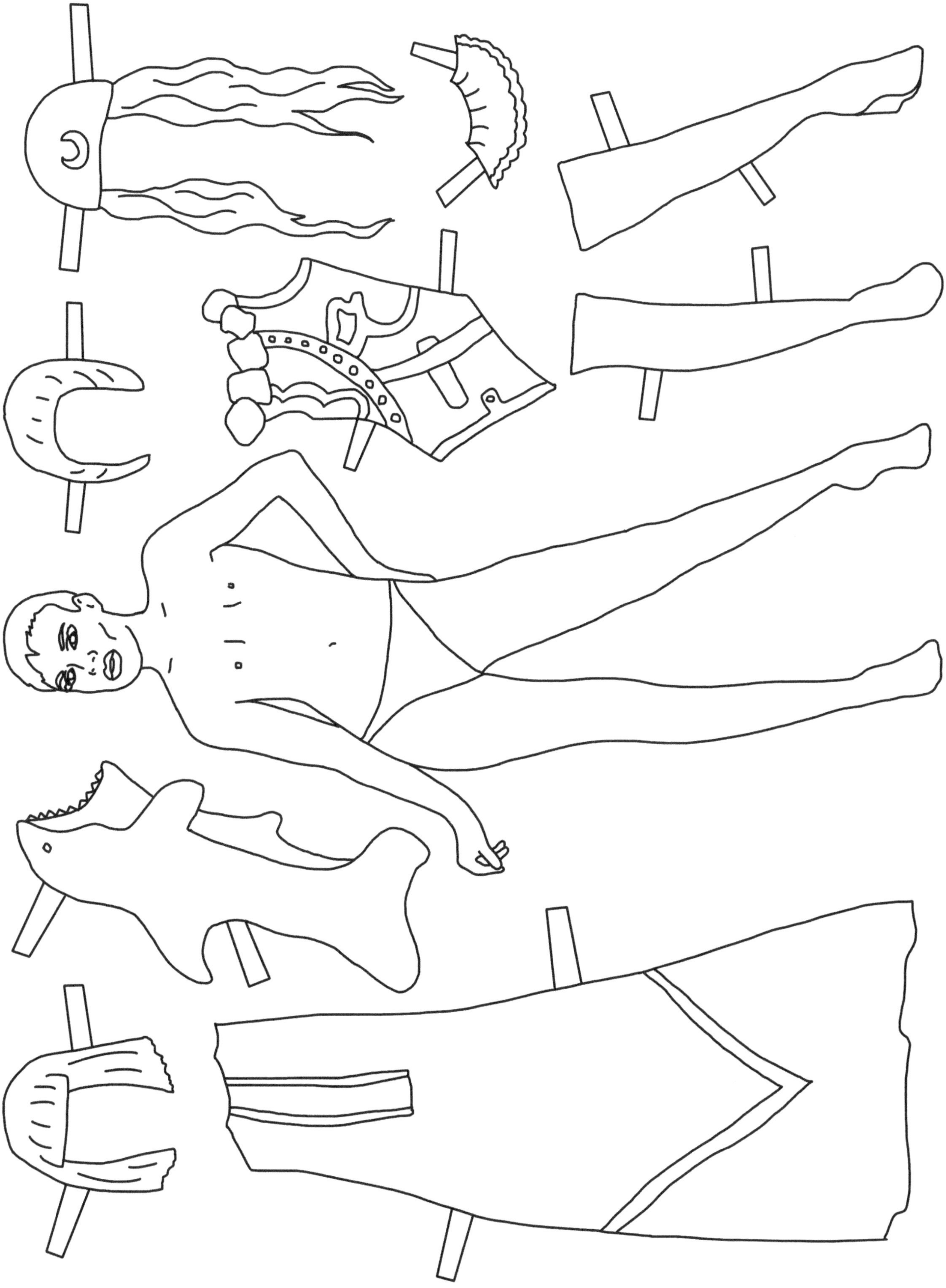

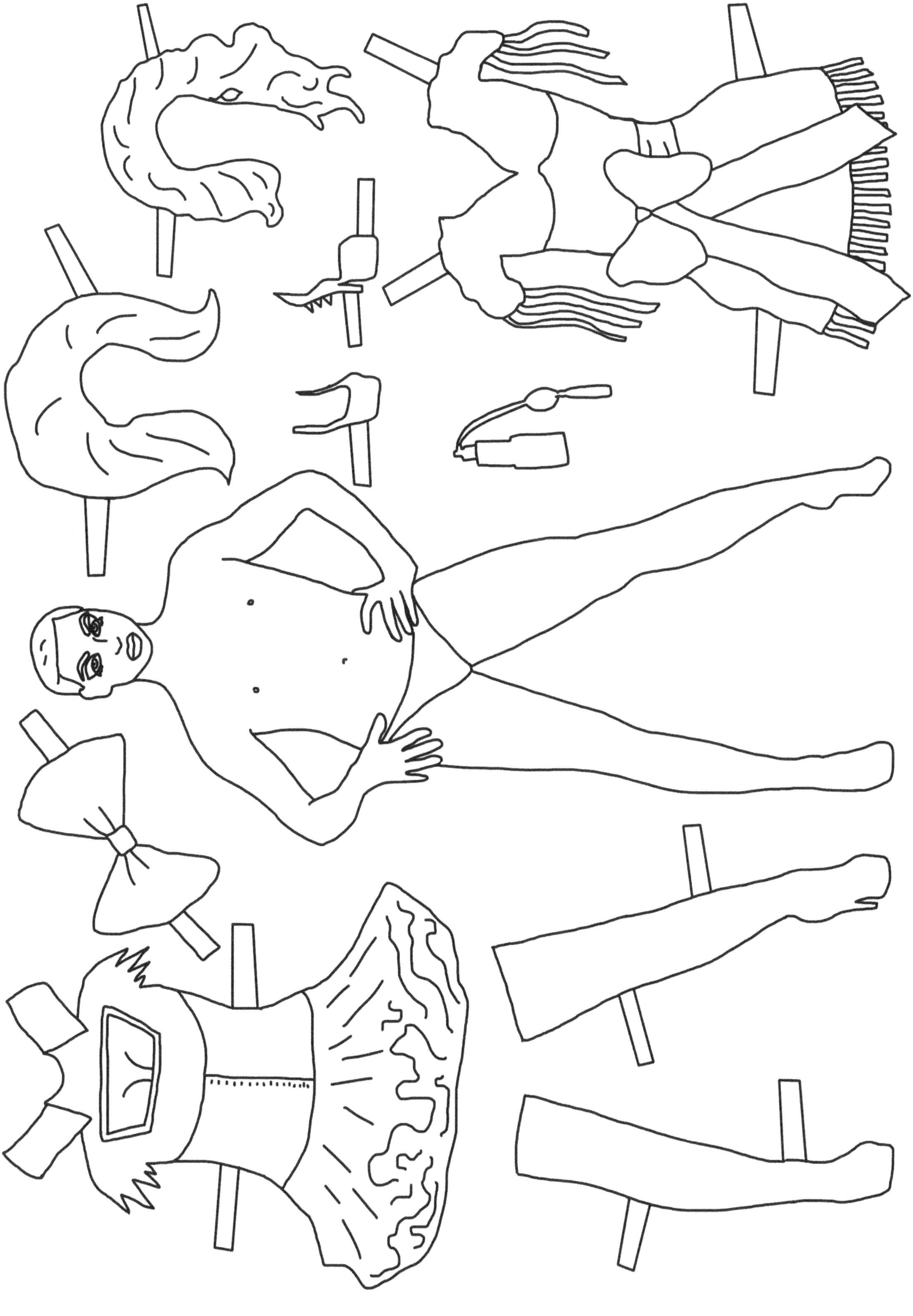

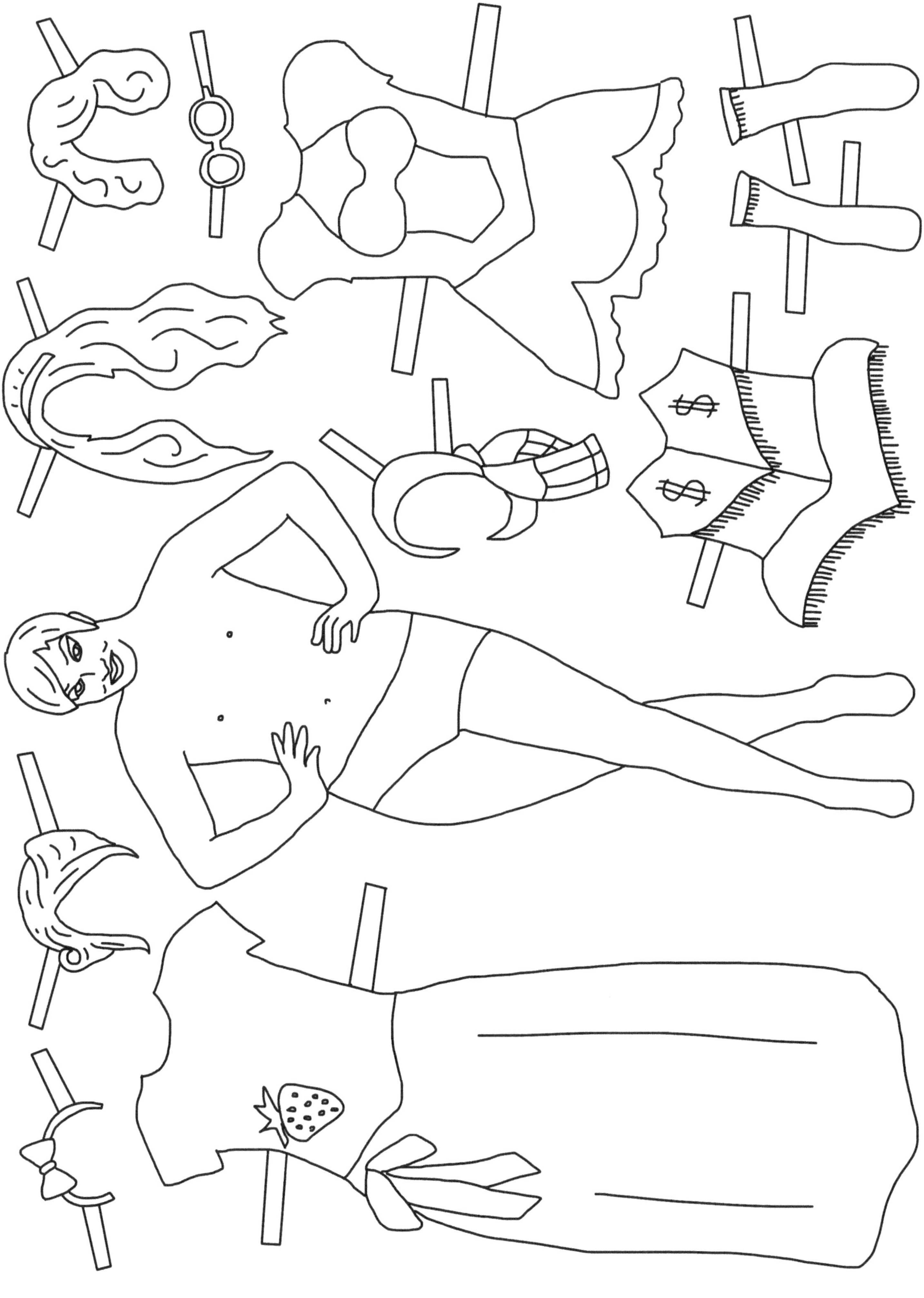

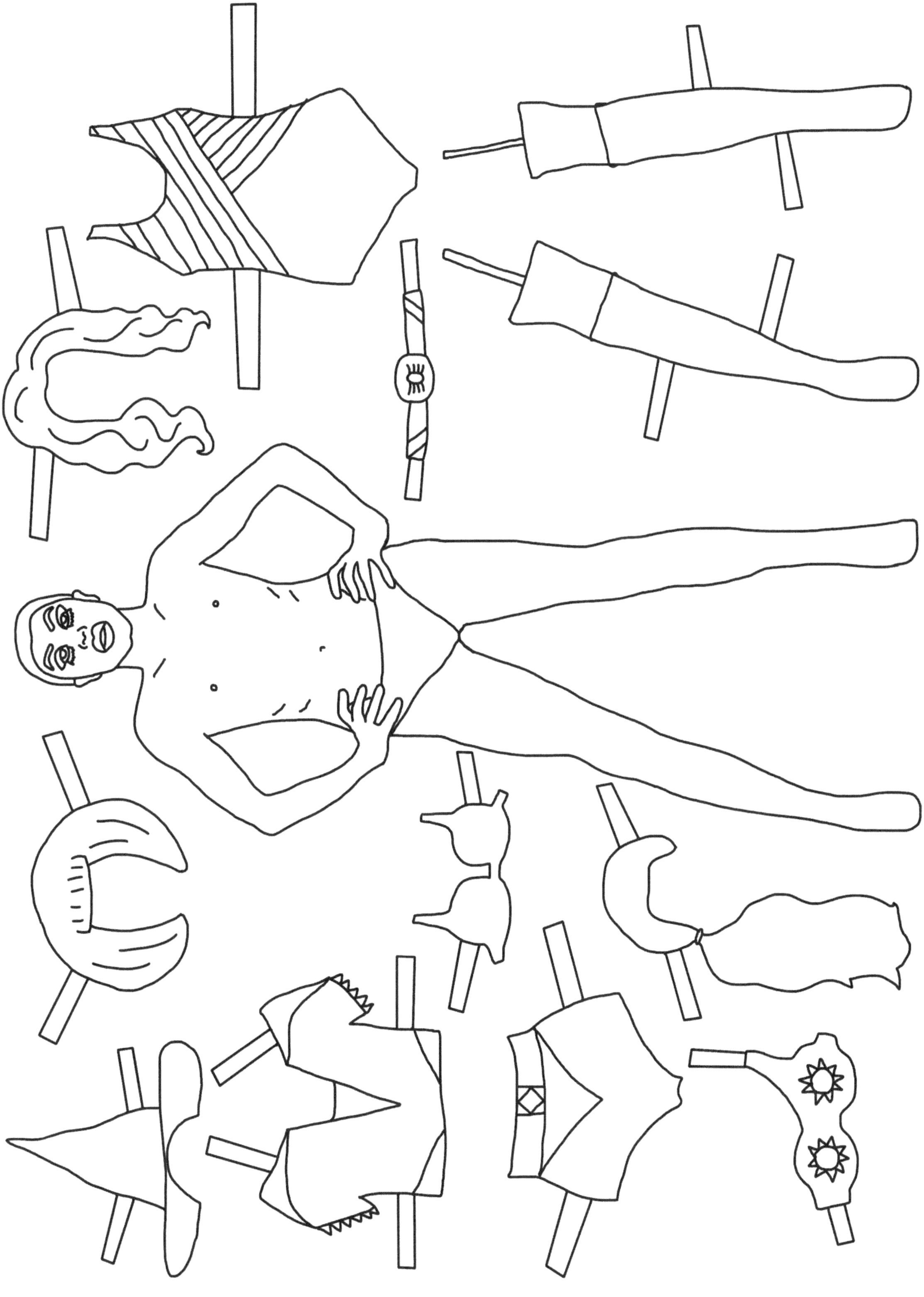

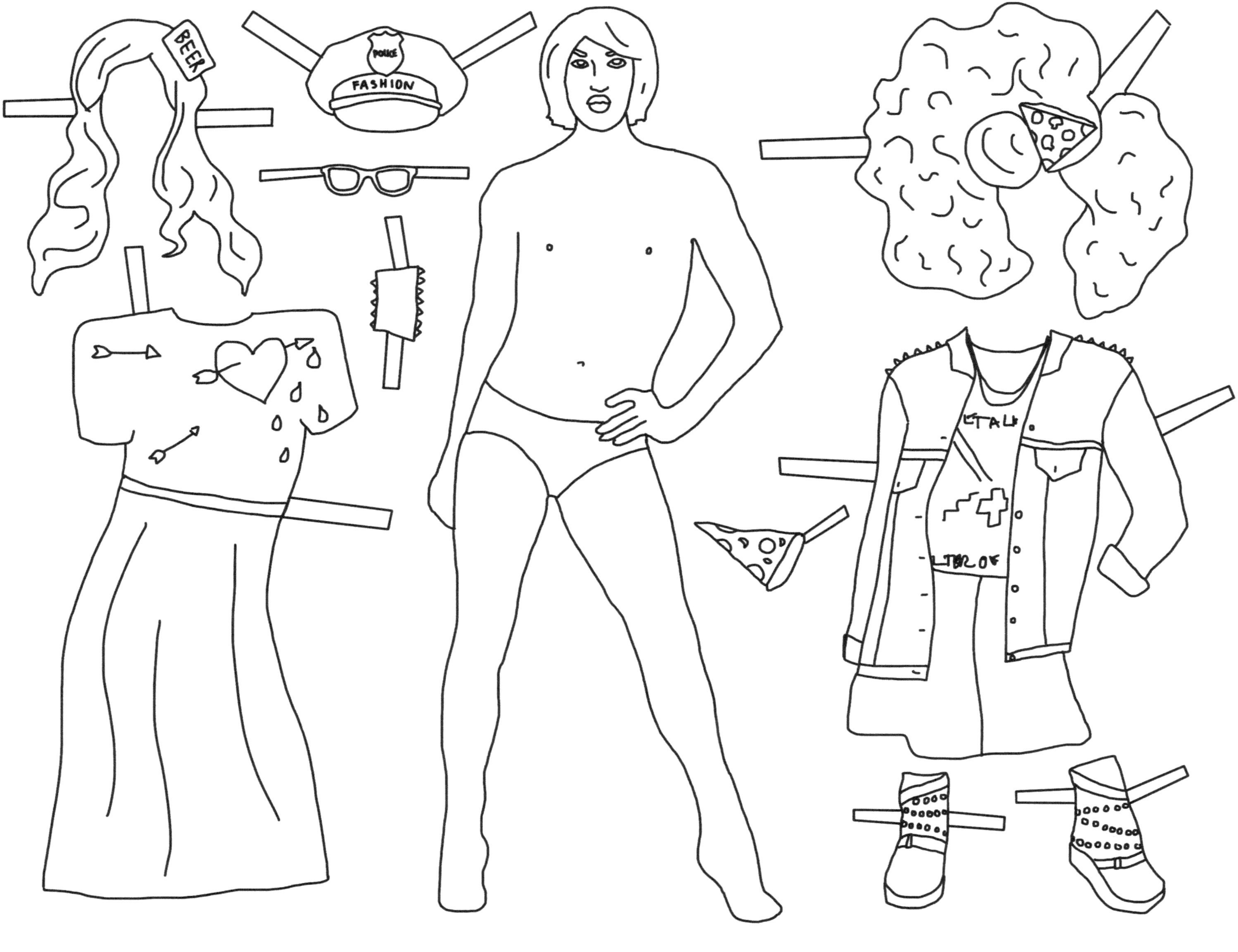
BEER
POLICE
FASHION

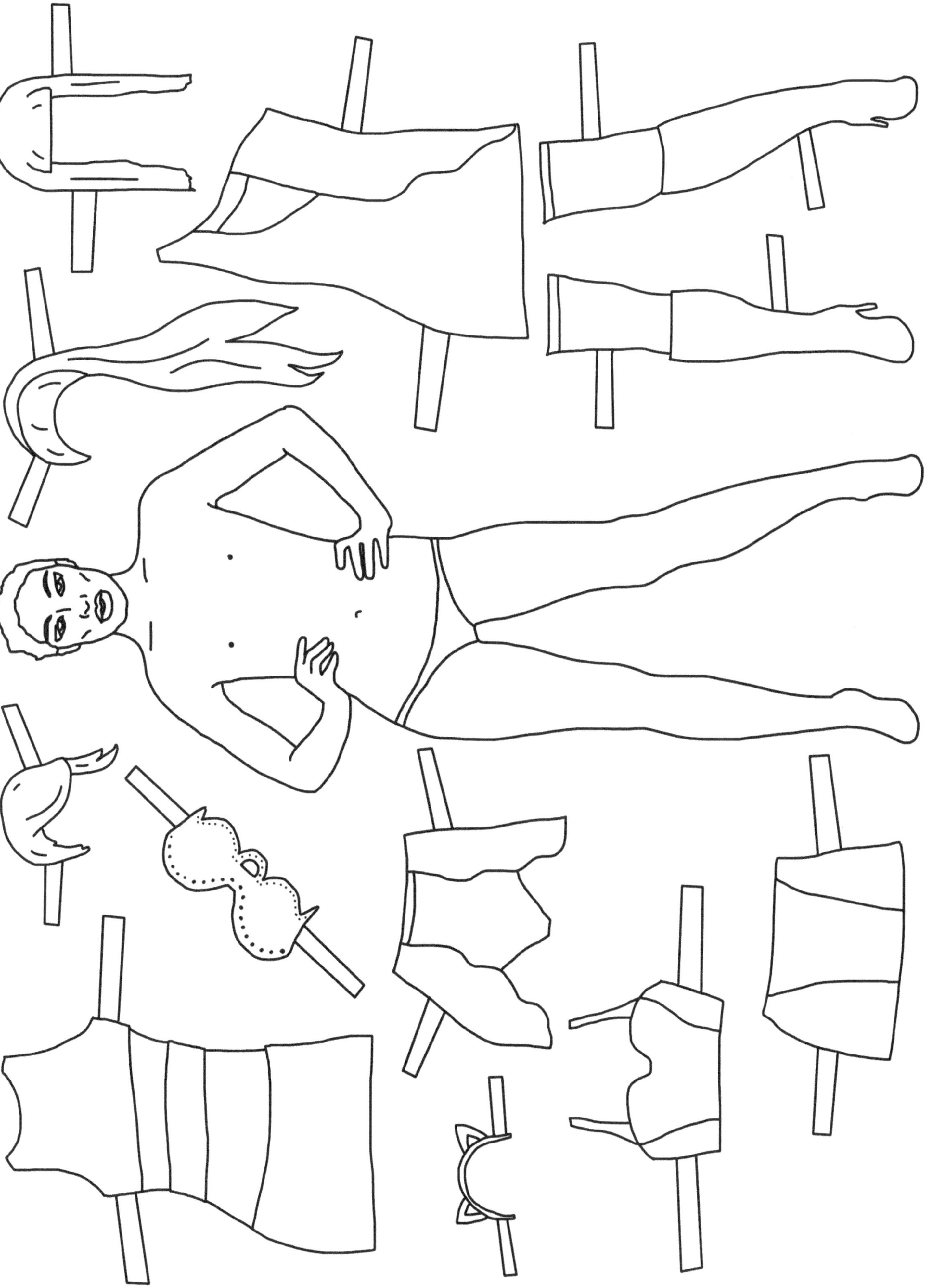

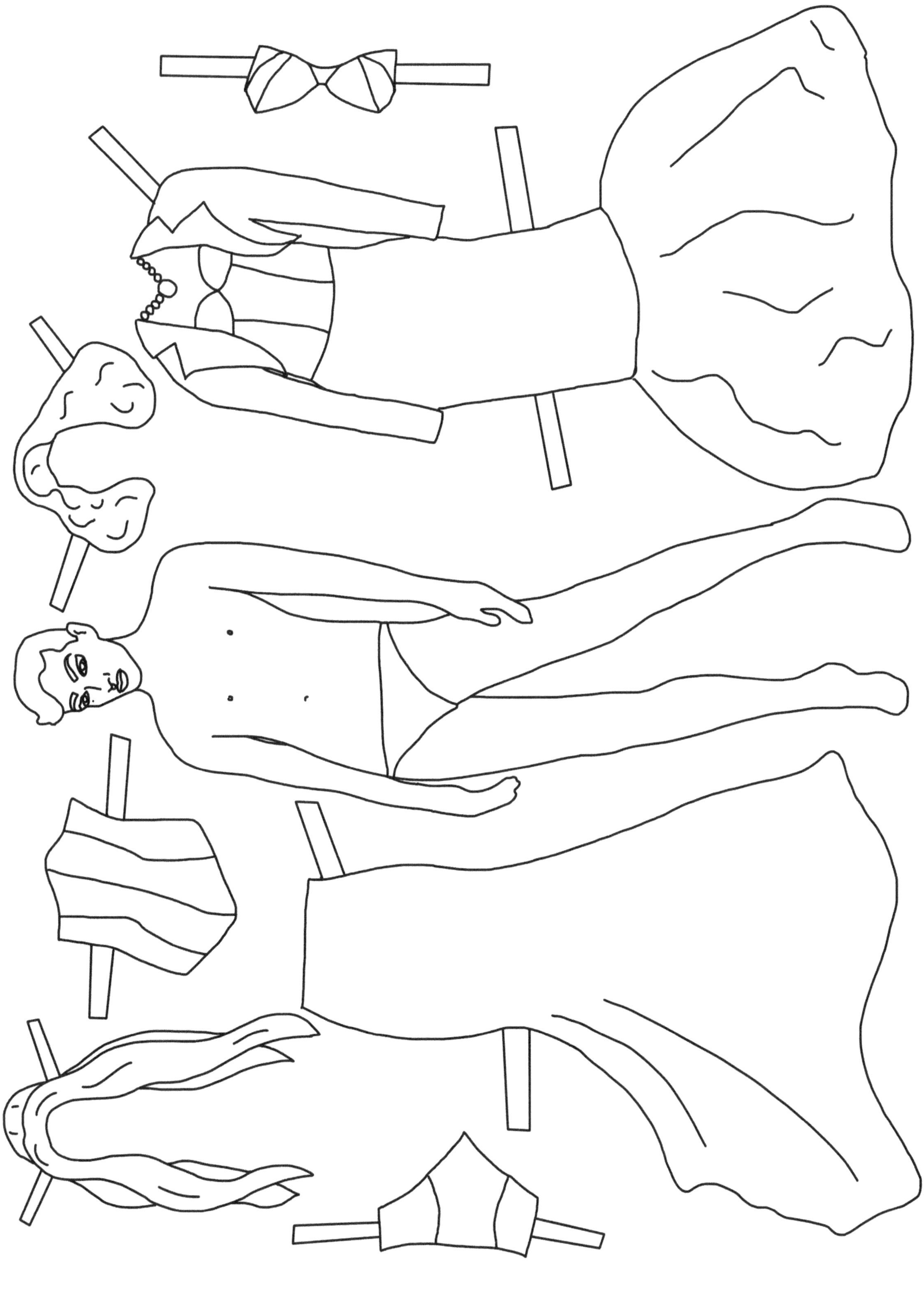

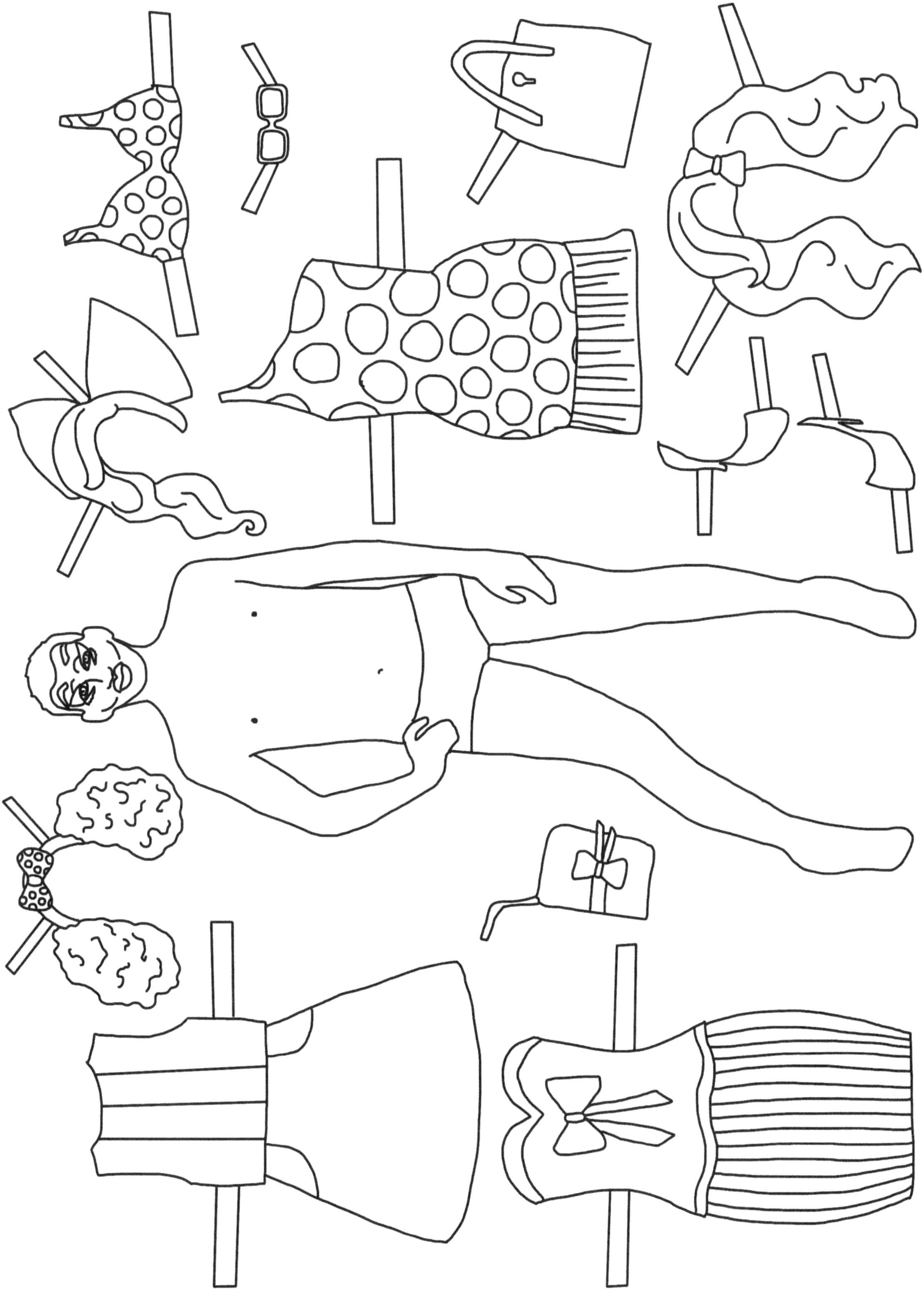

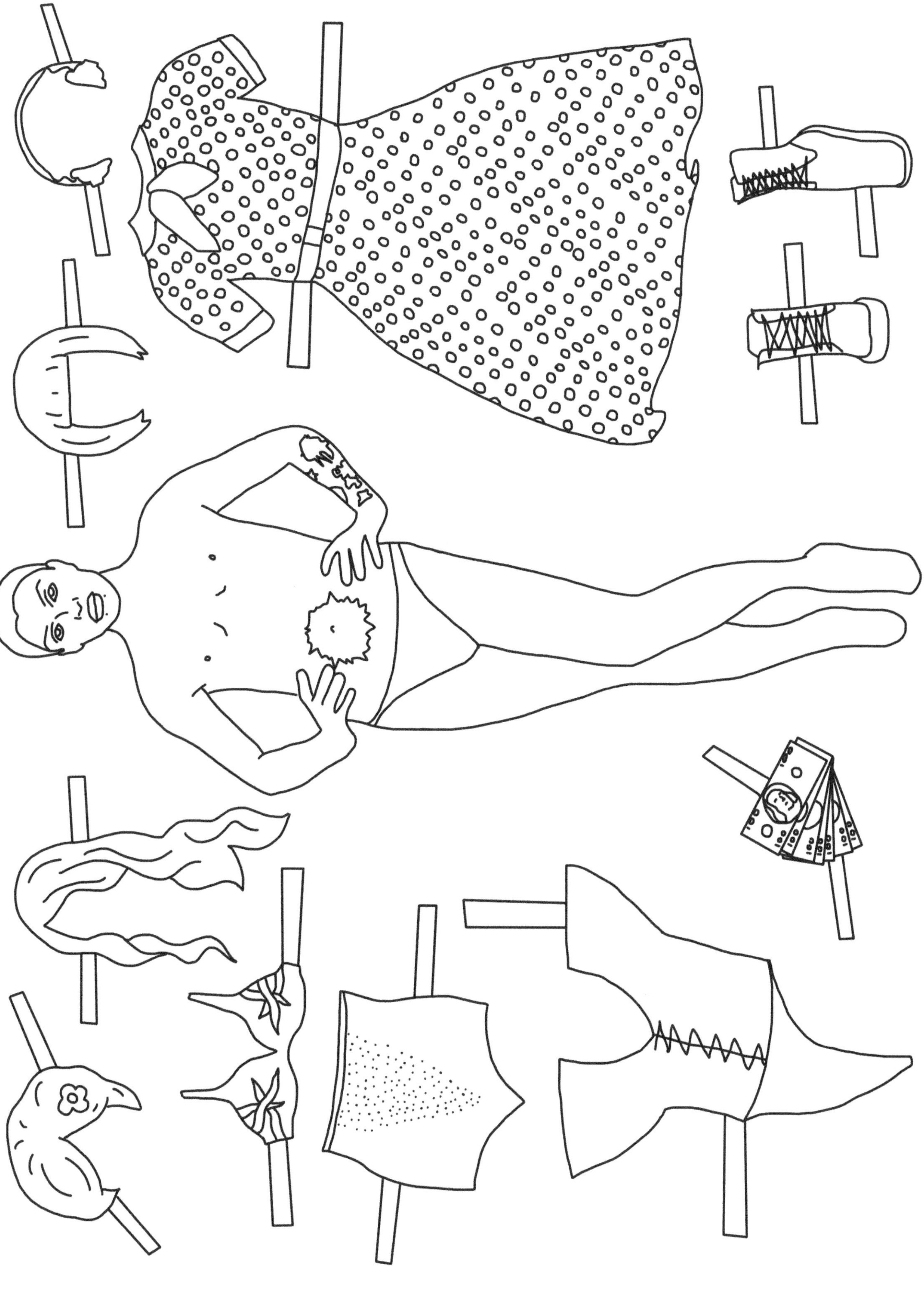

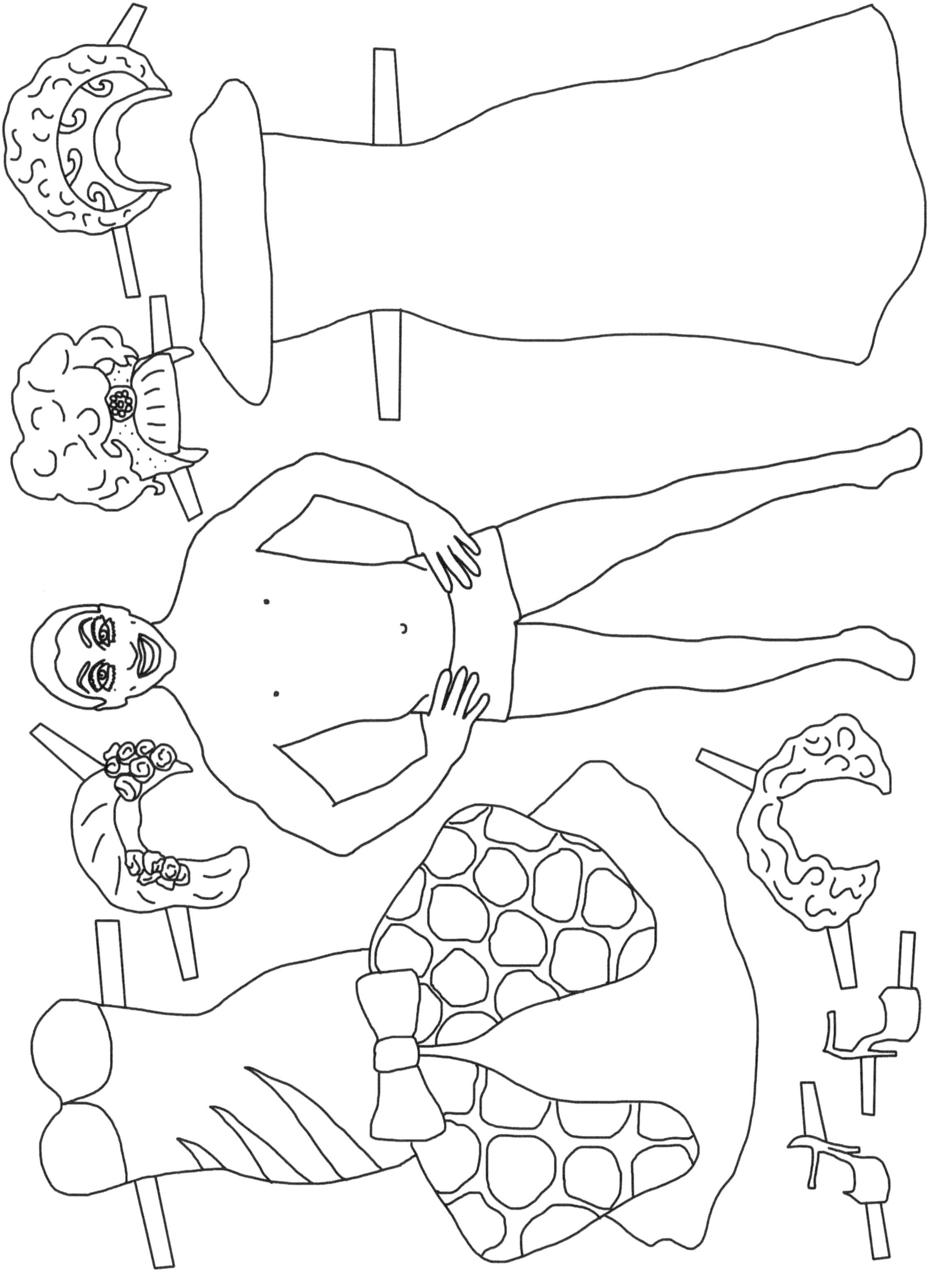

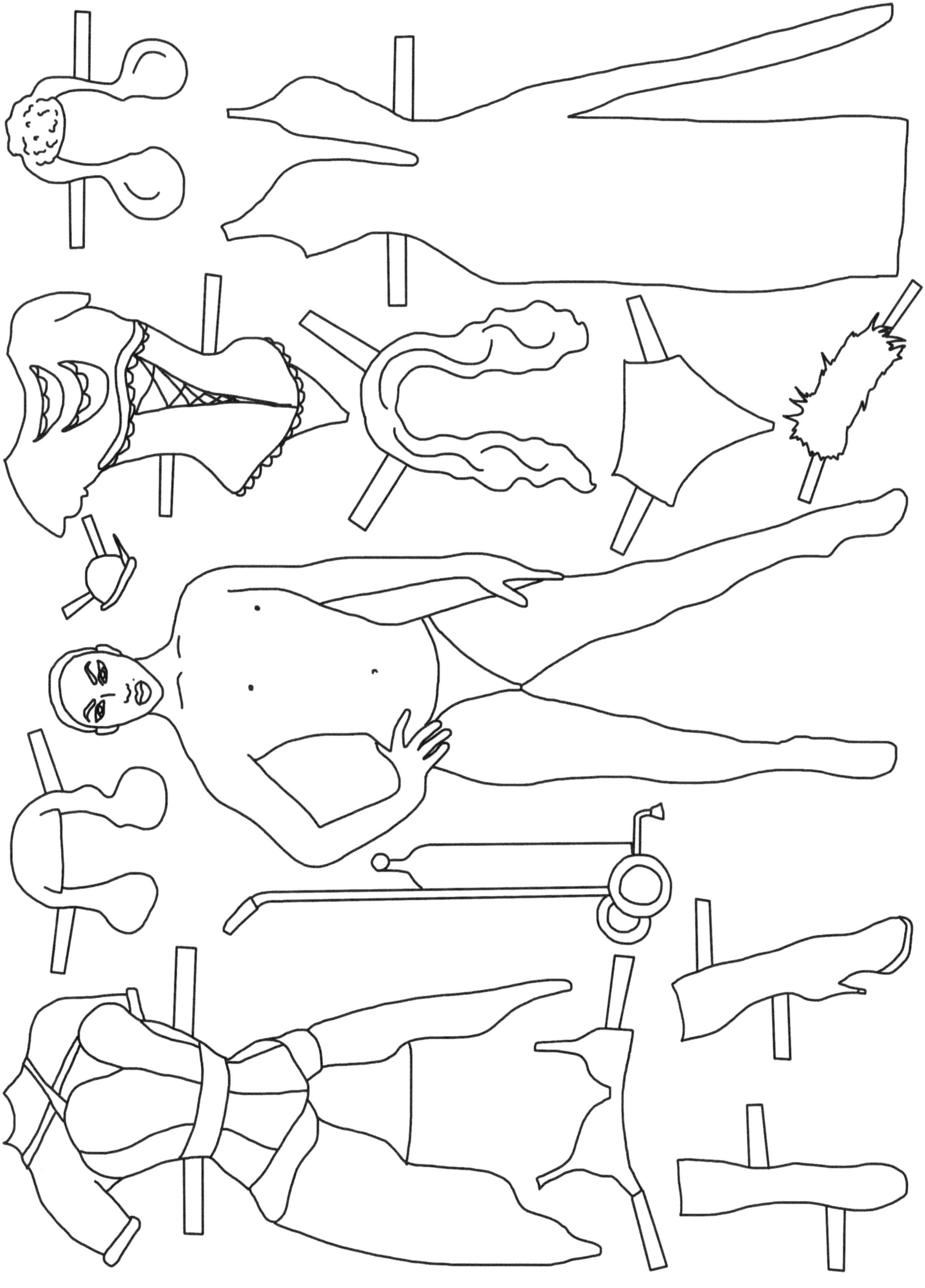

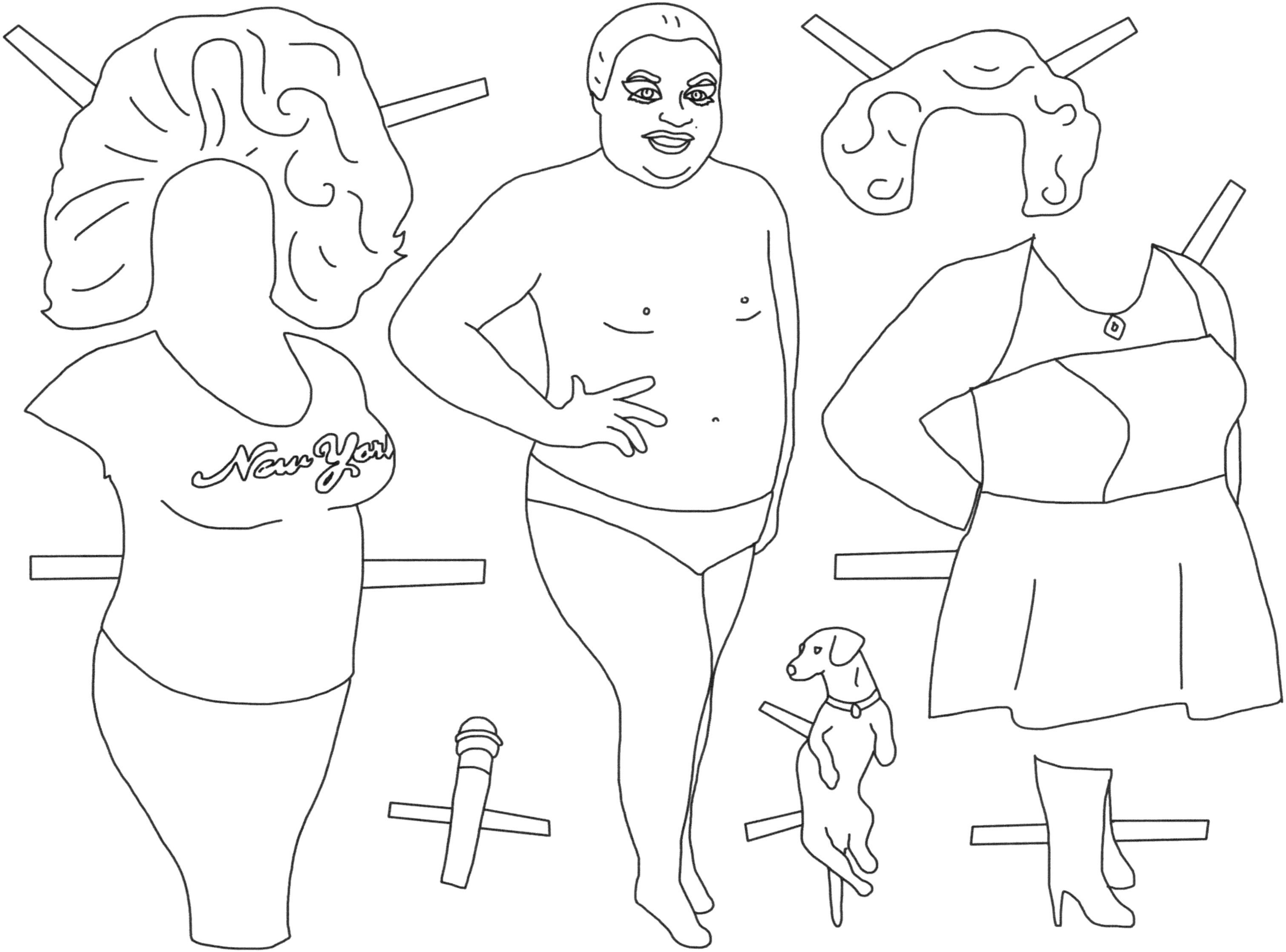
New York

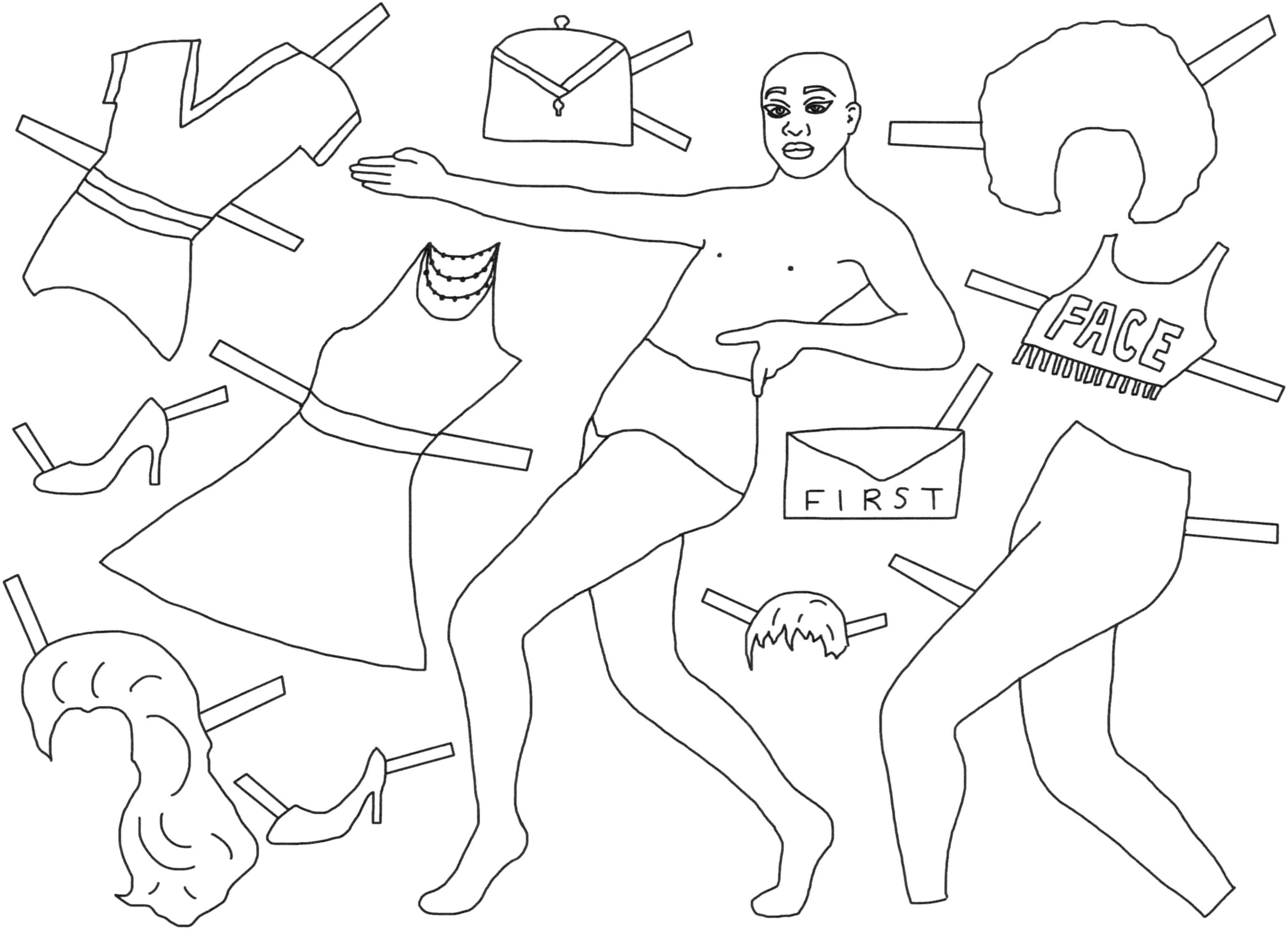
FACE
FIRST

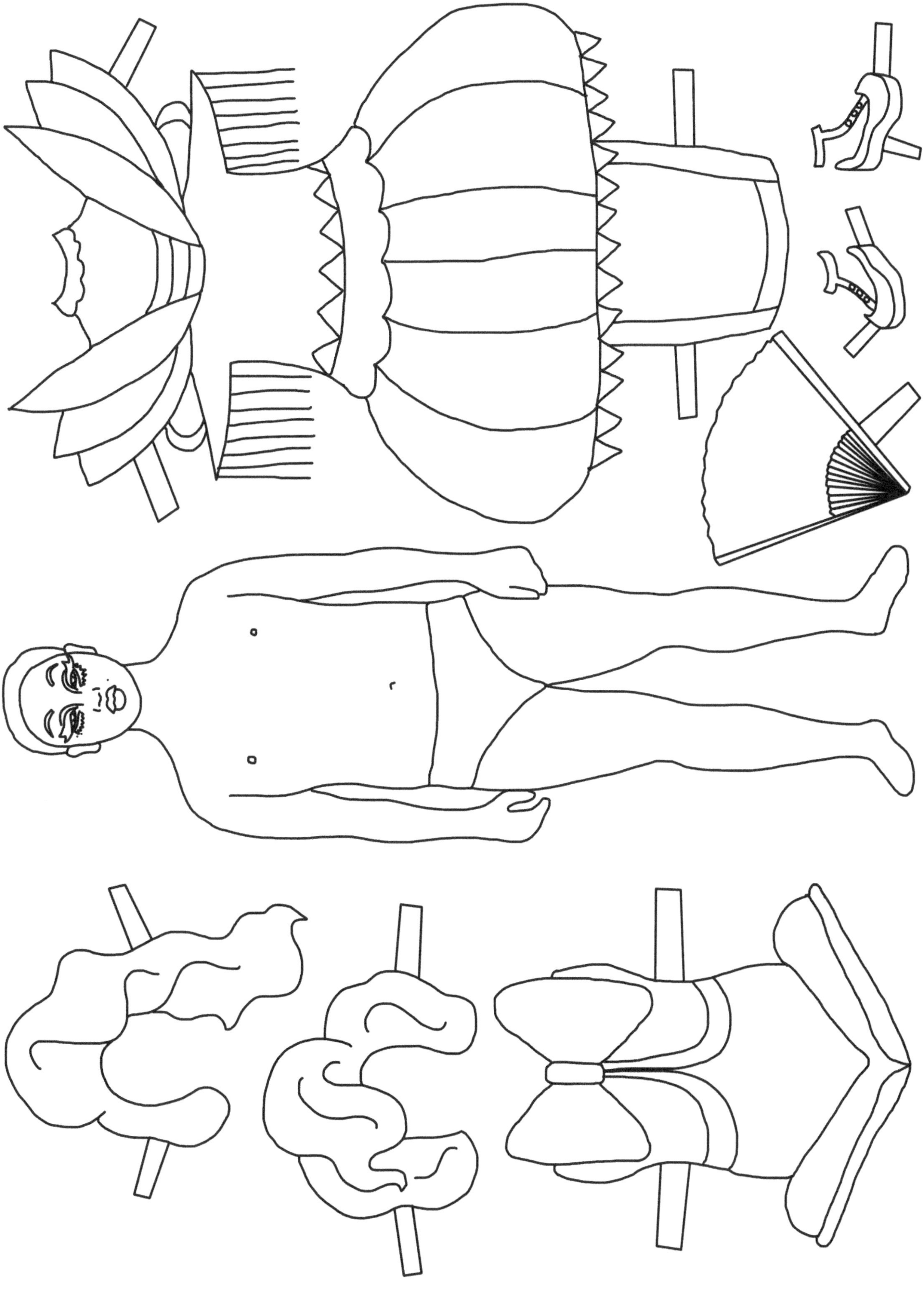

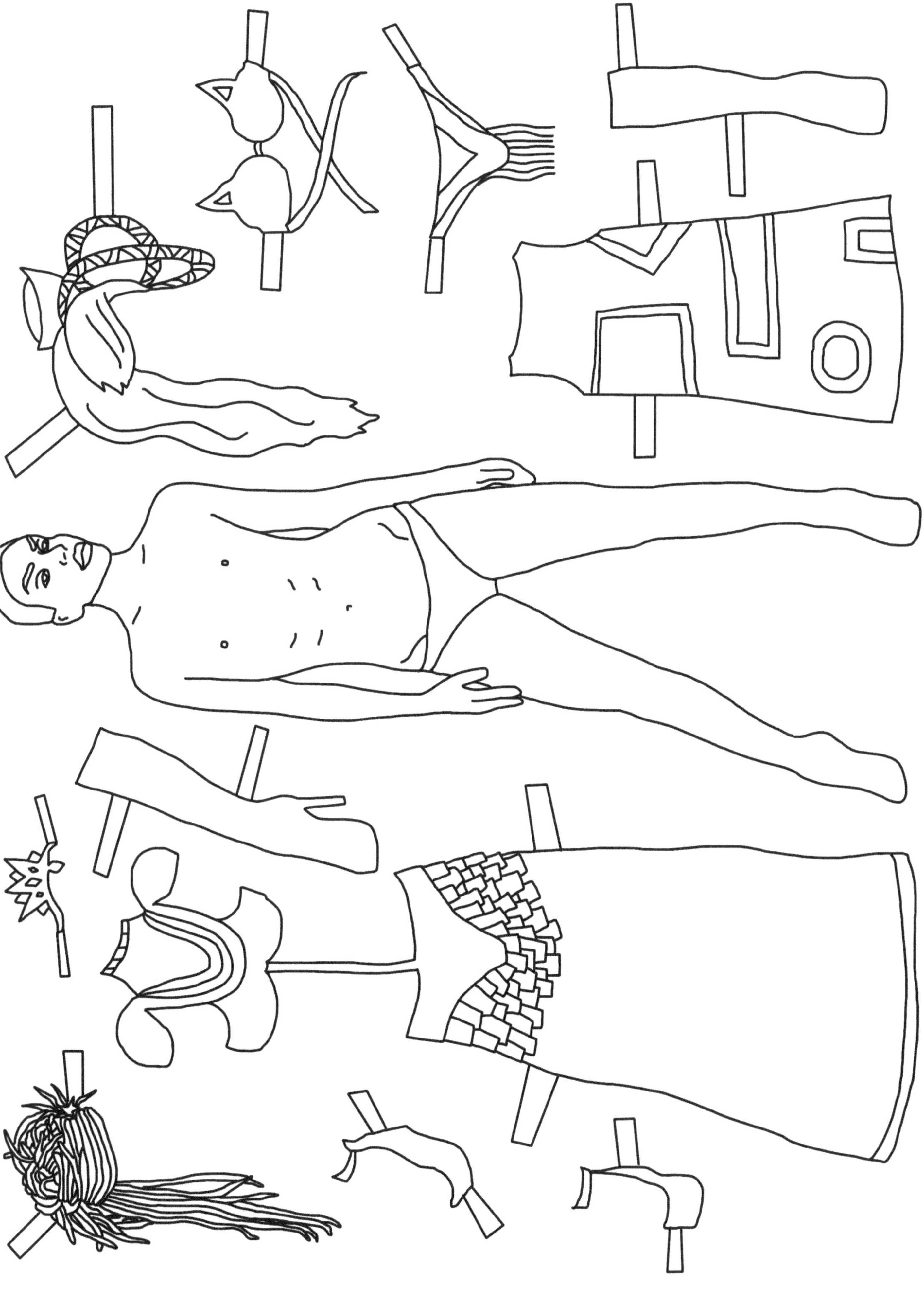

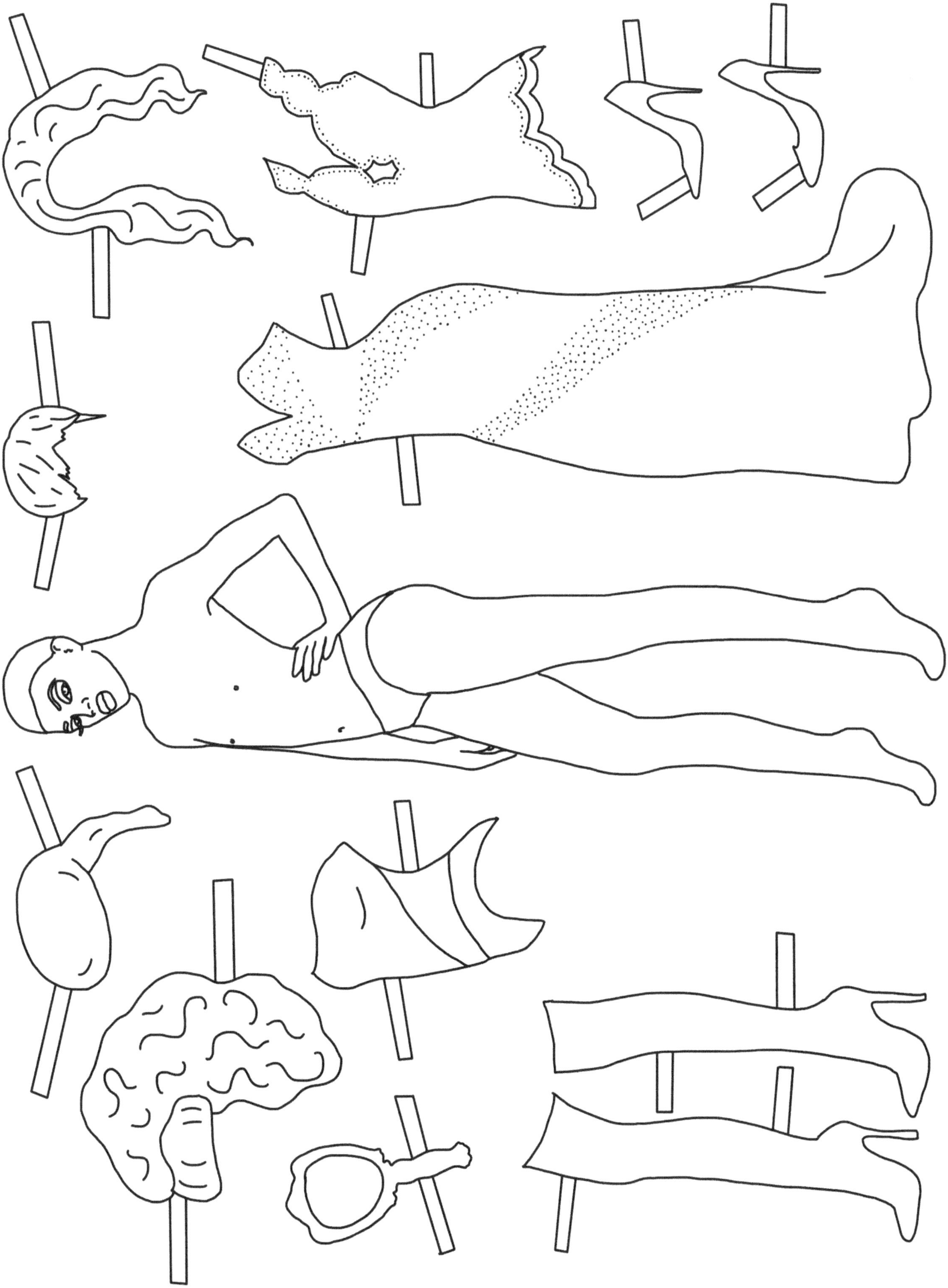

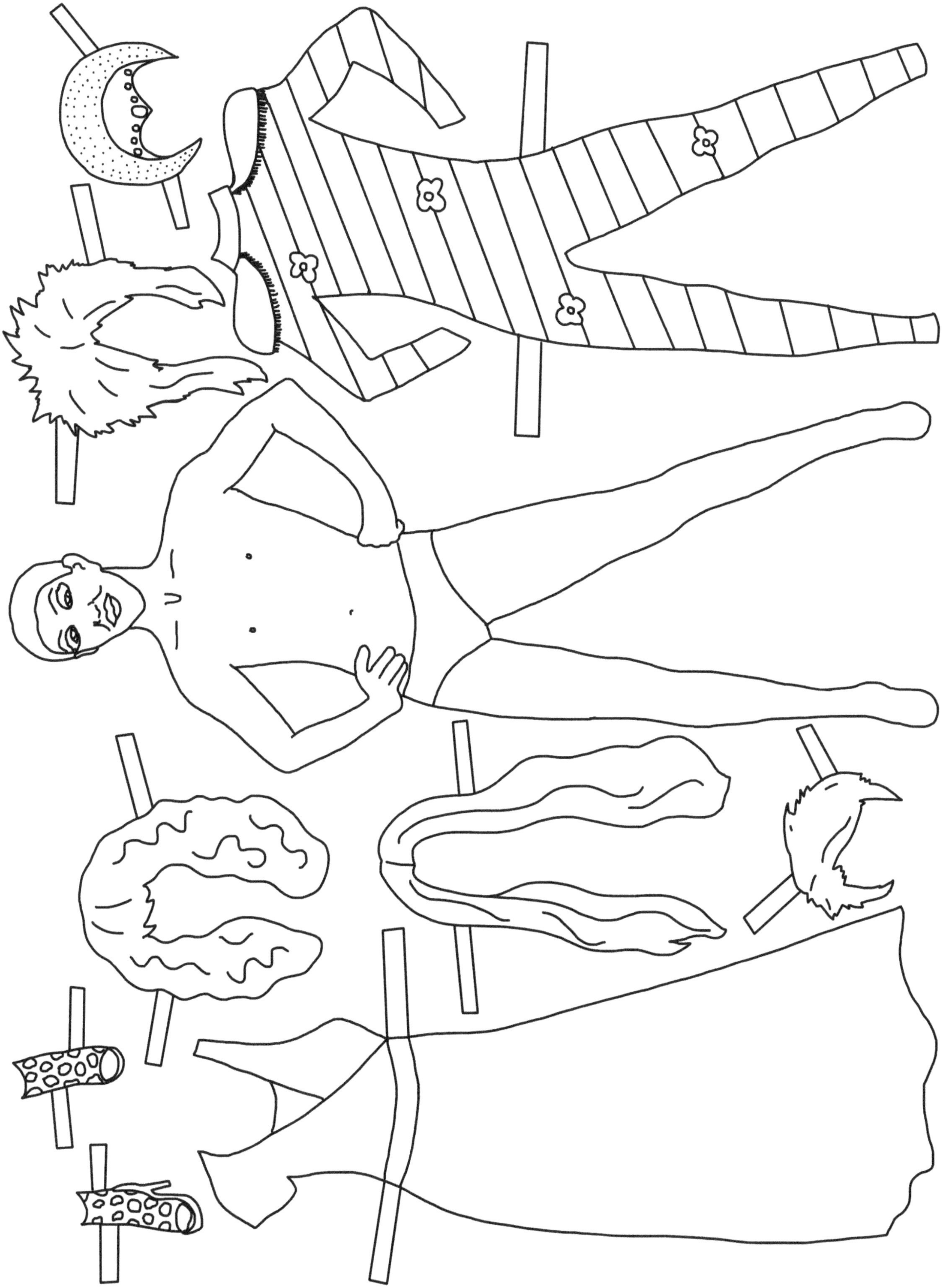

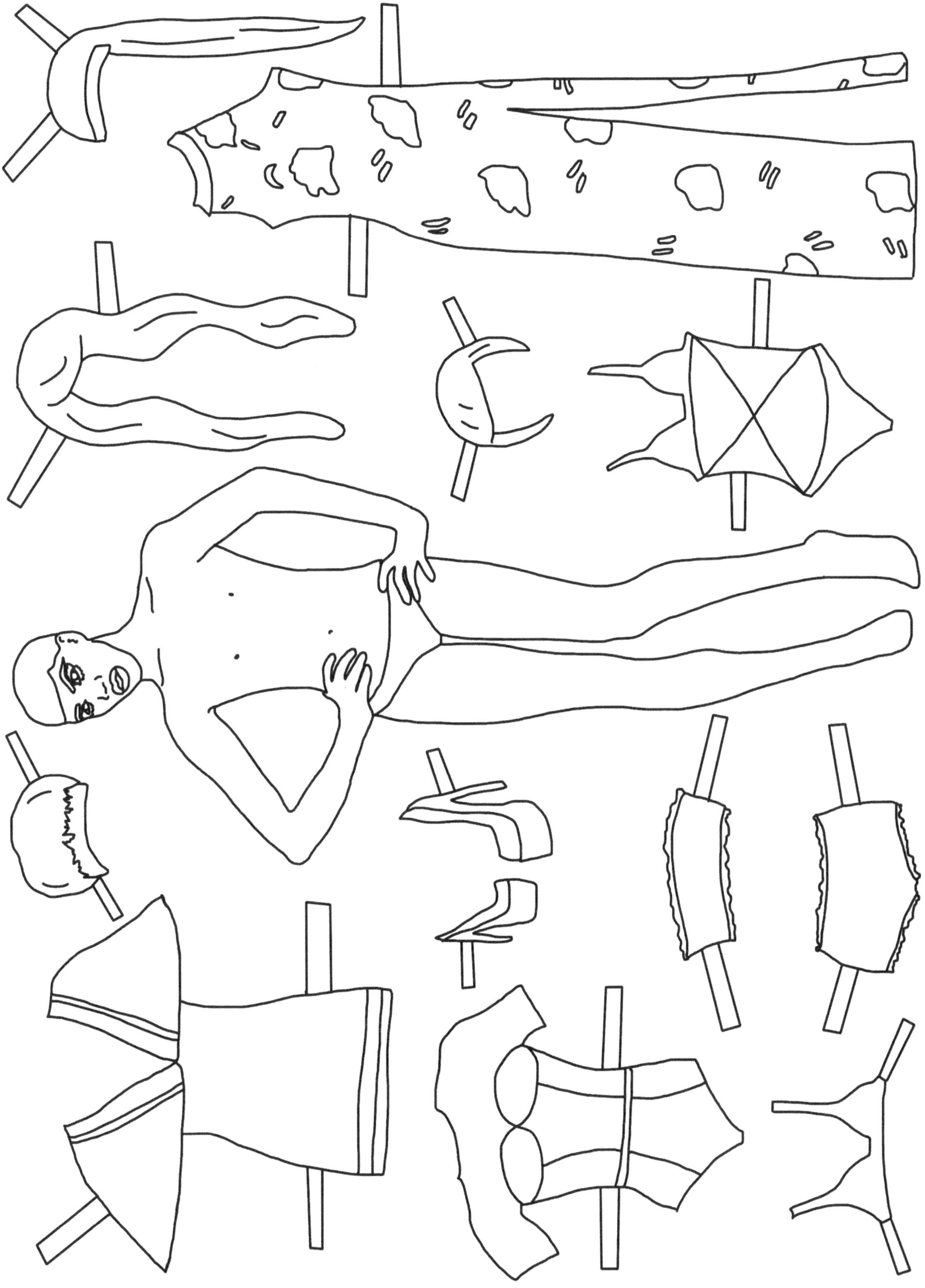

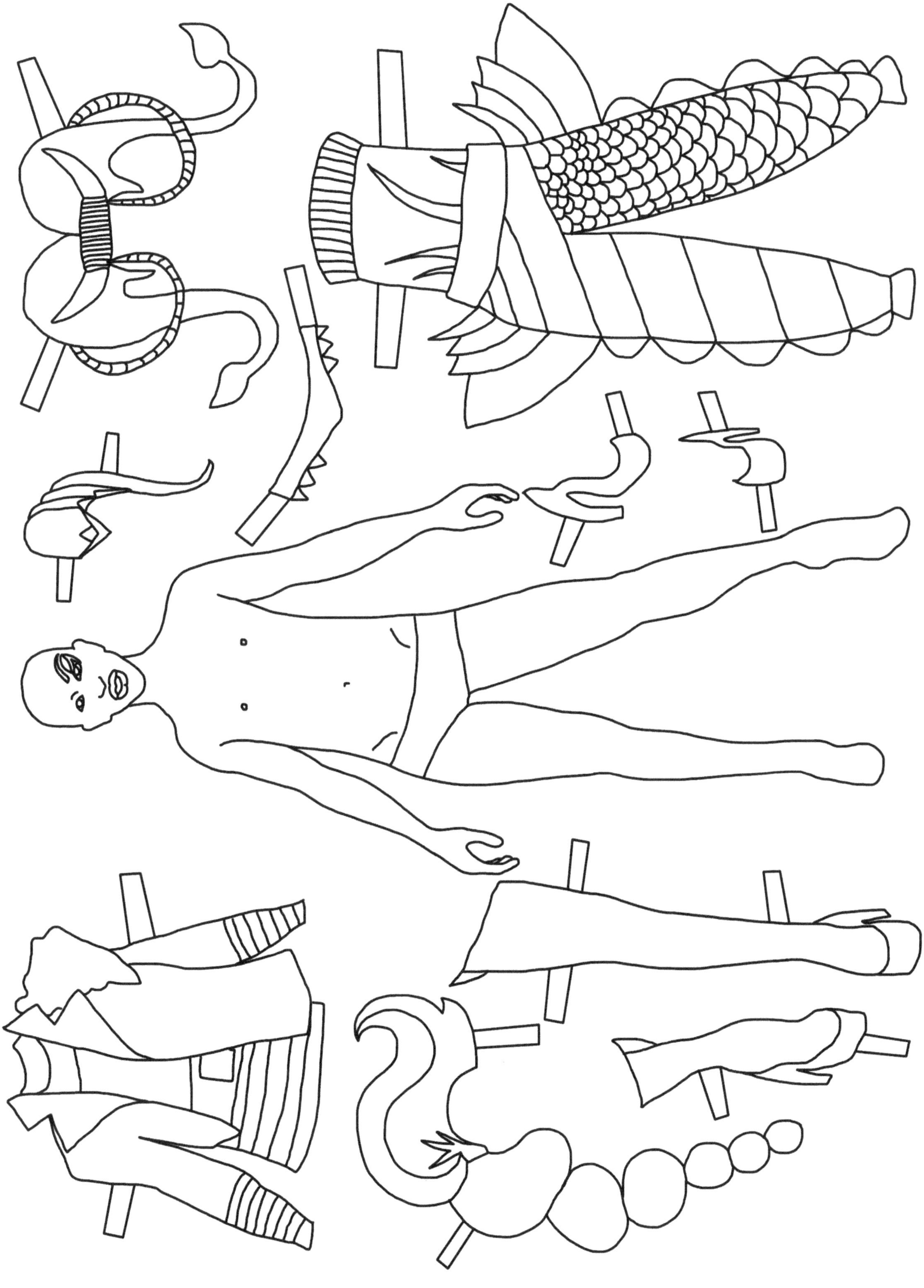

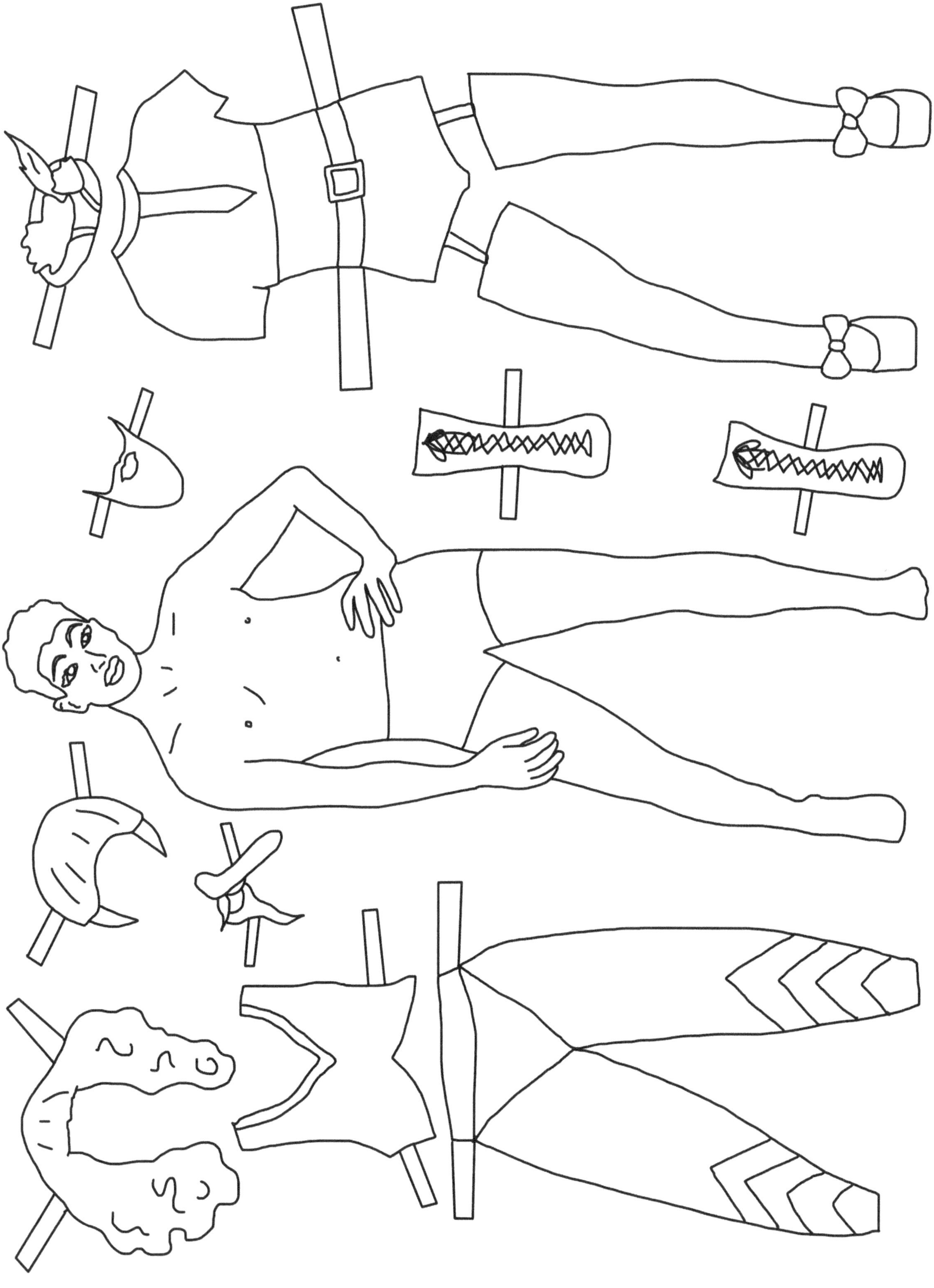

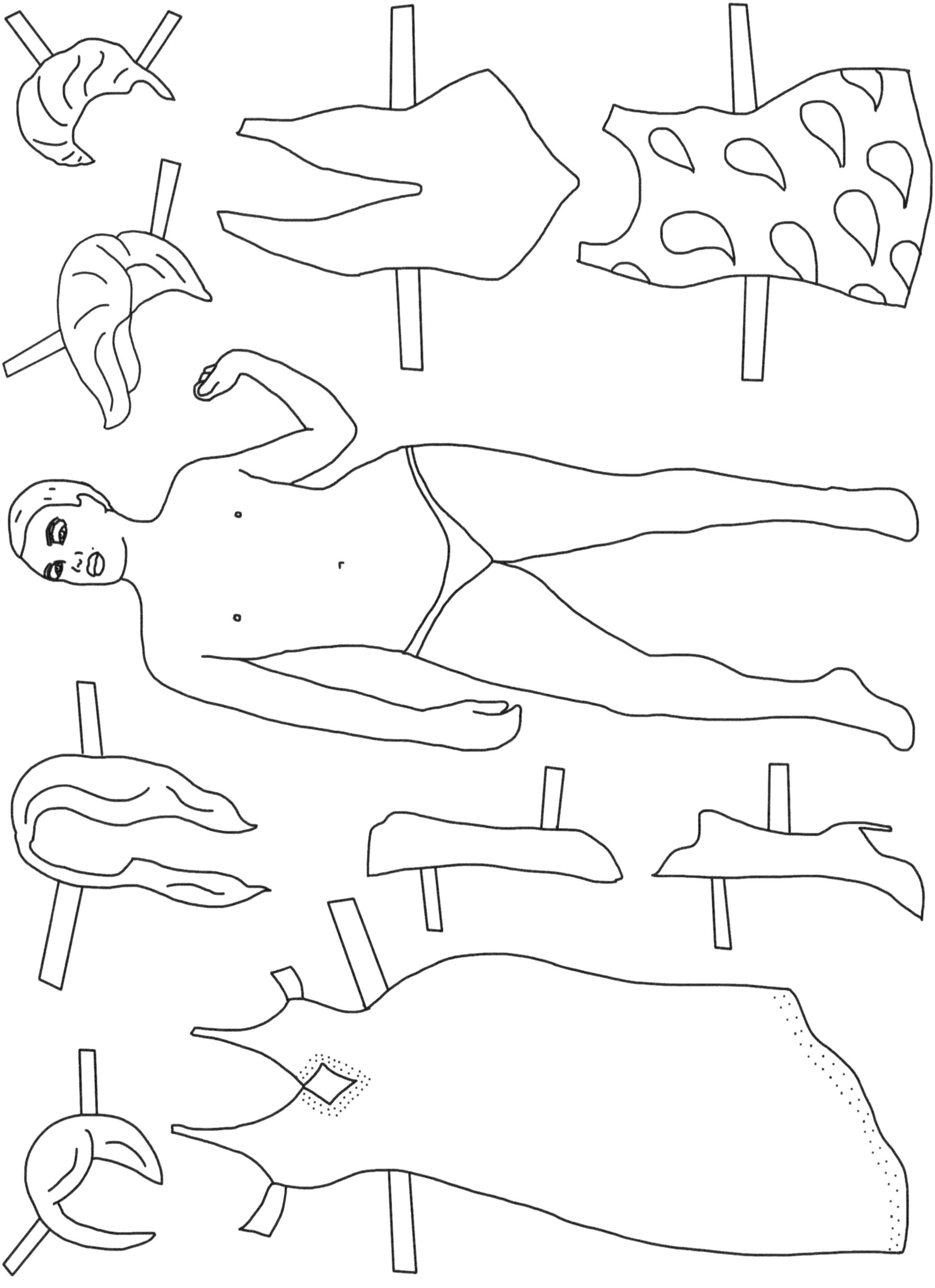

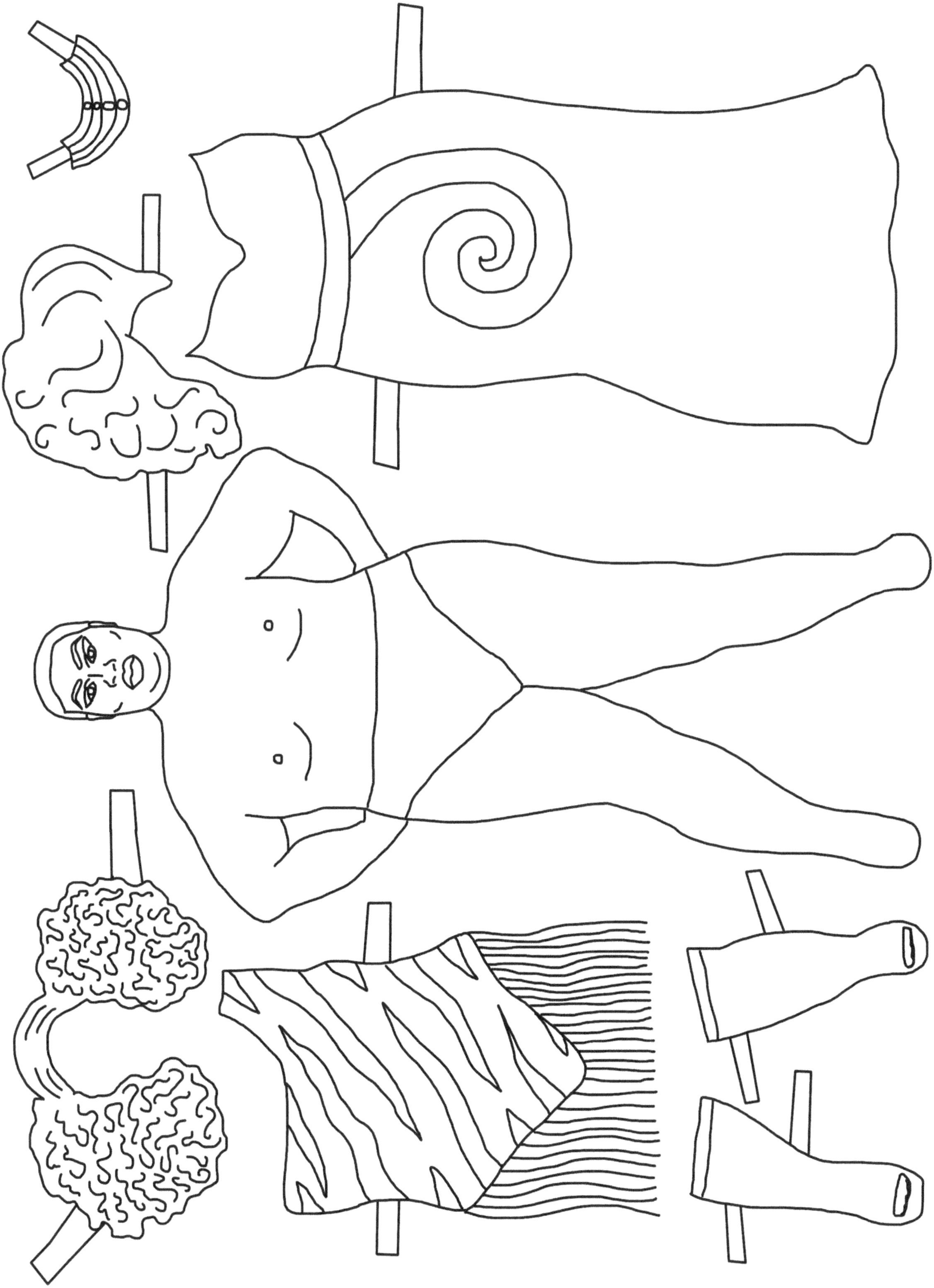

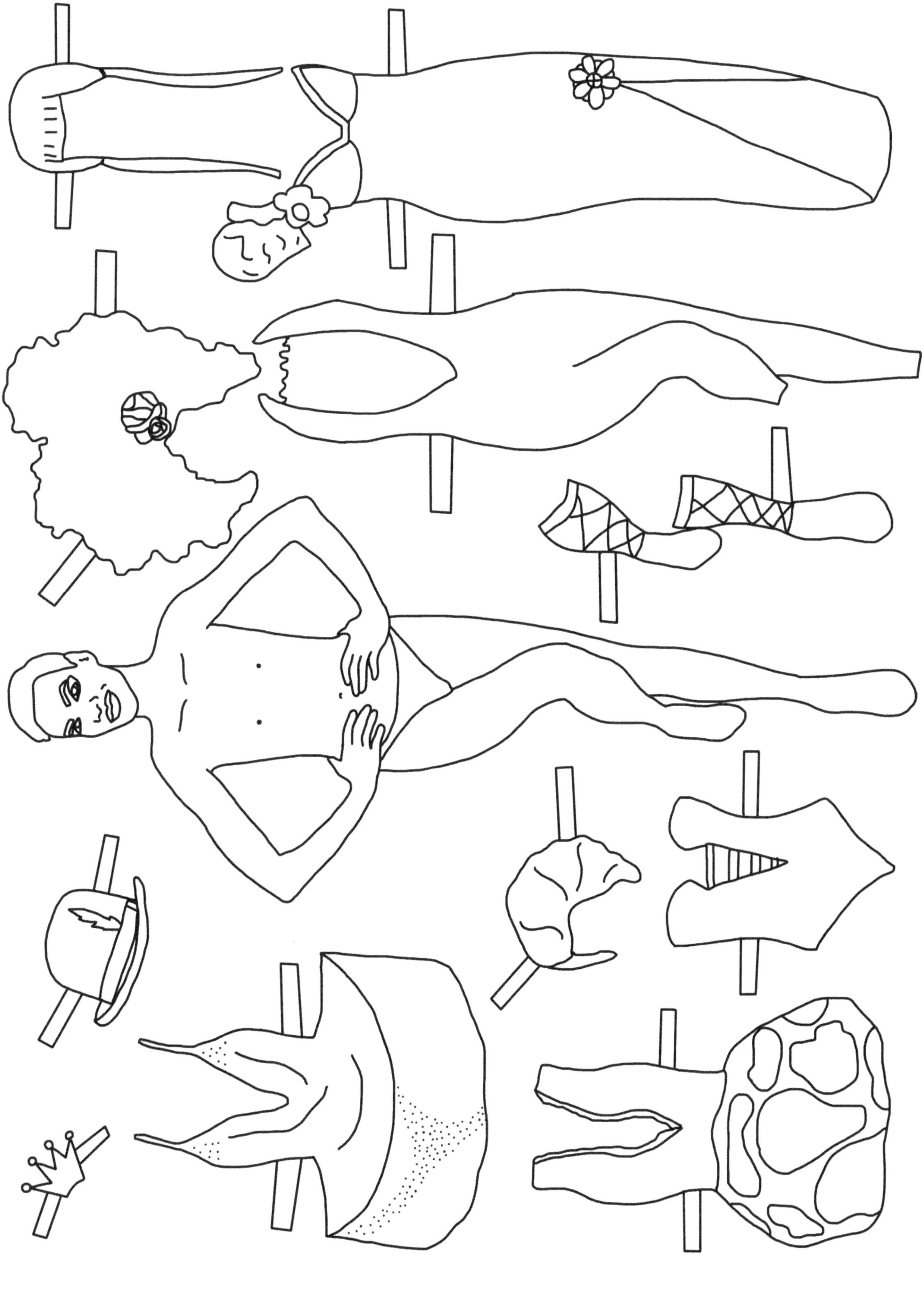

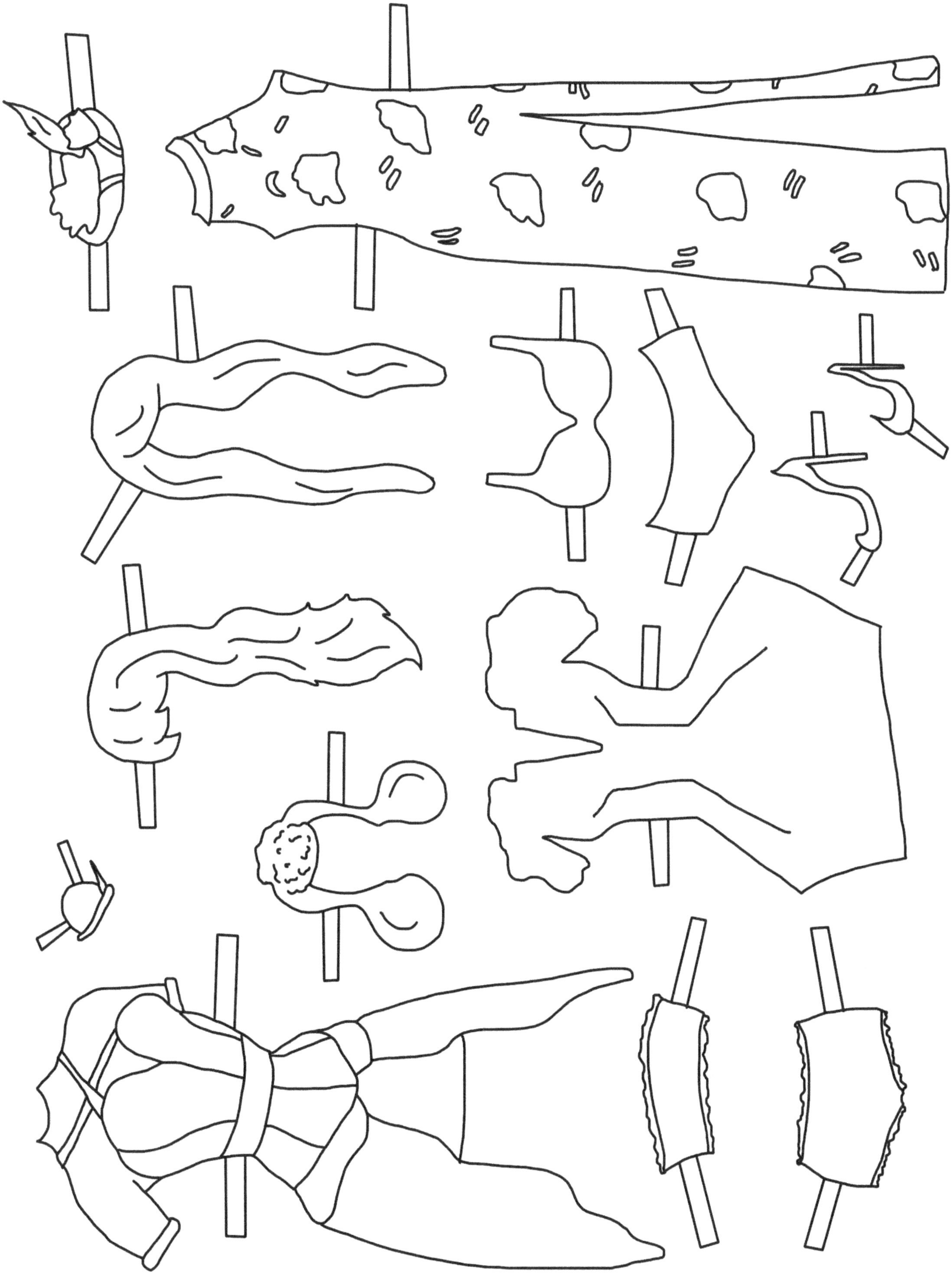

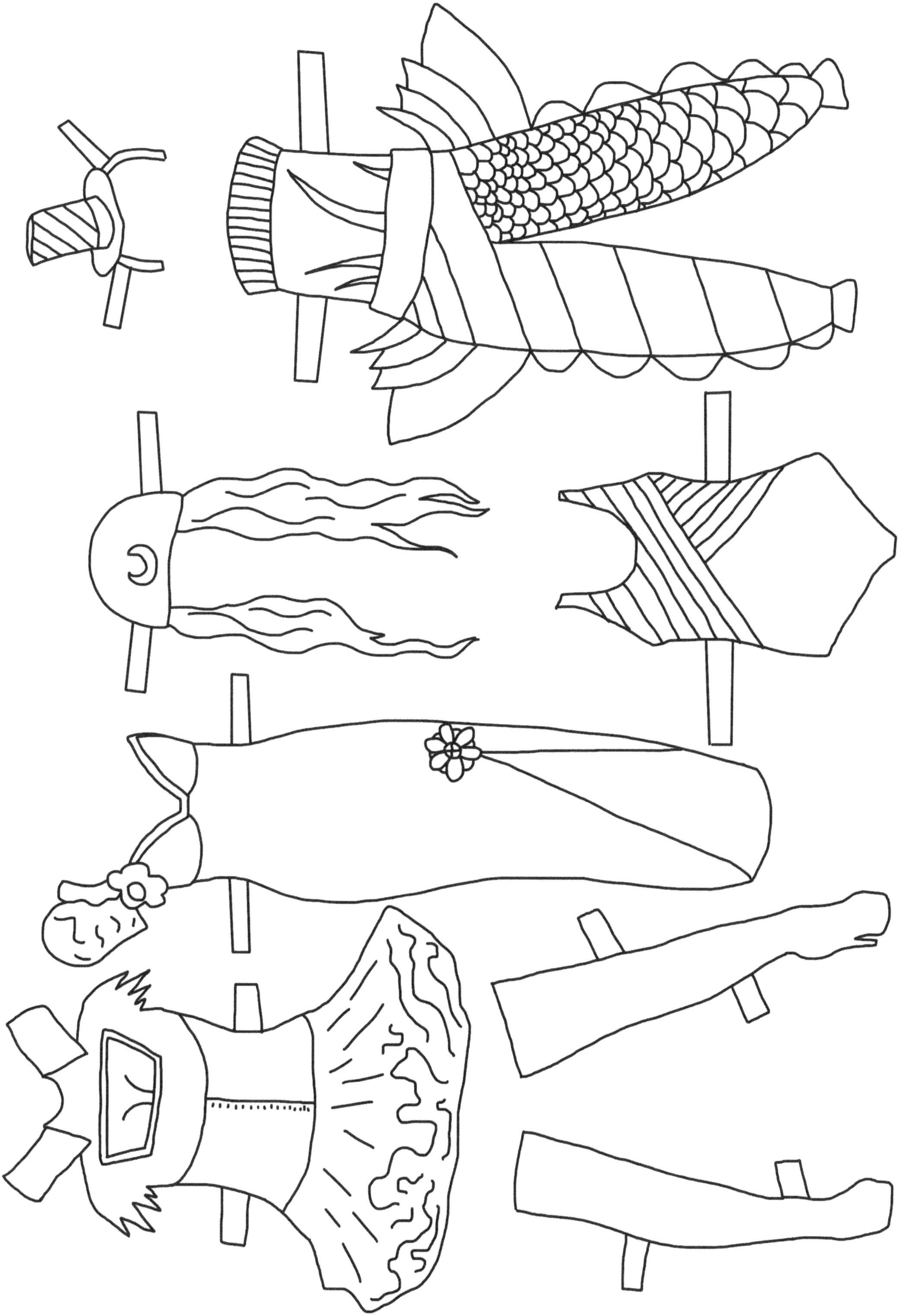

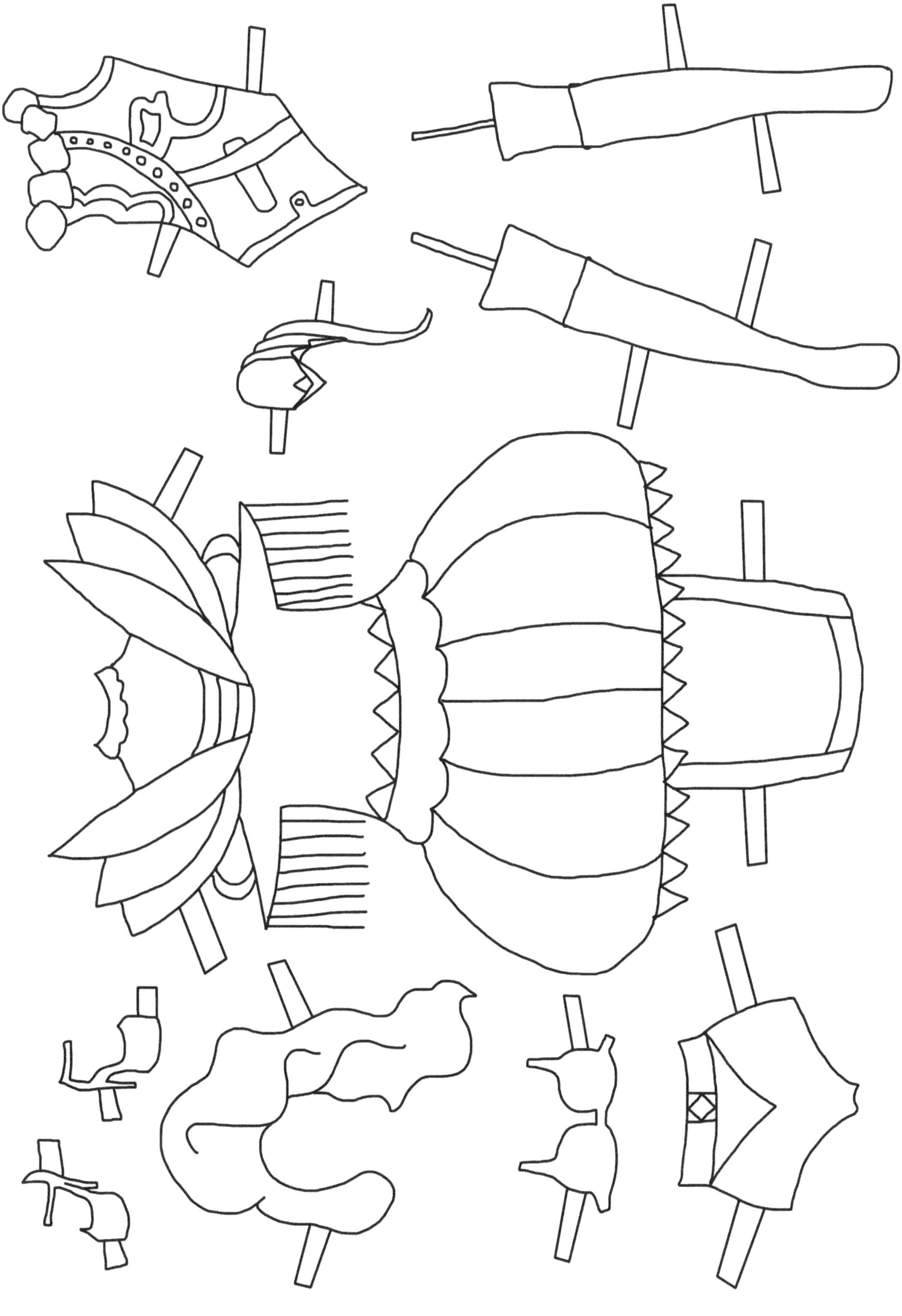

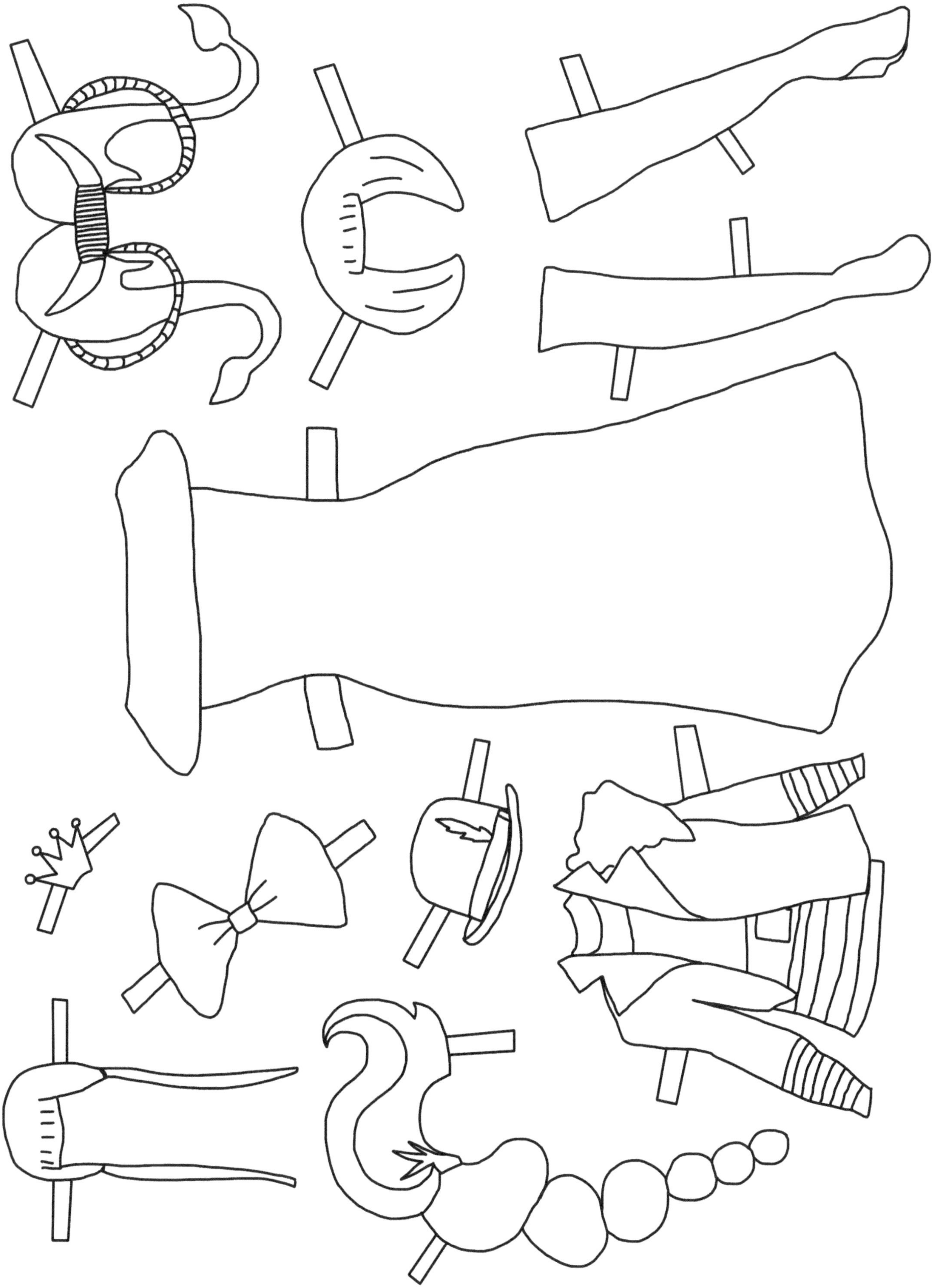

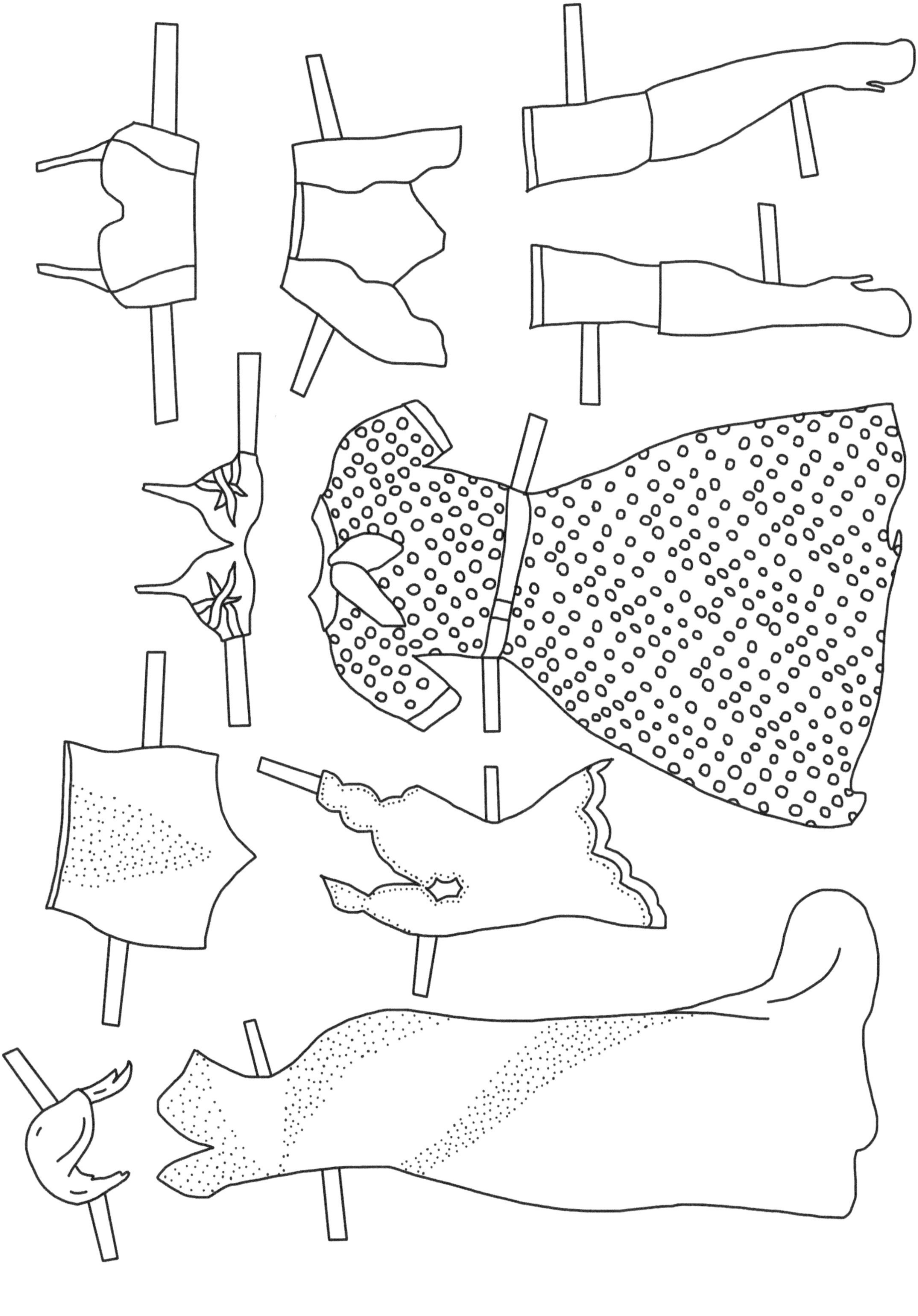

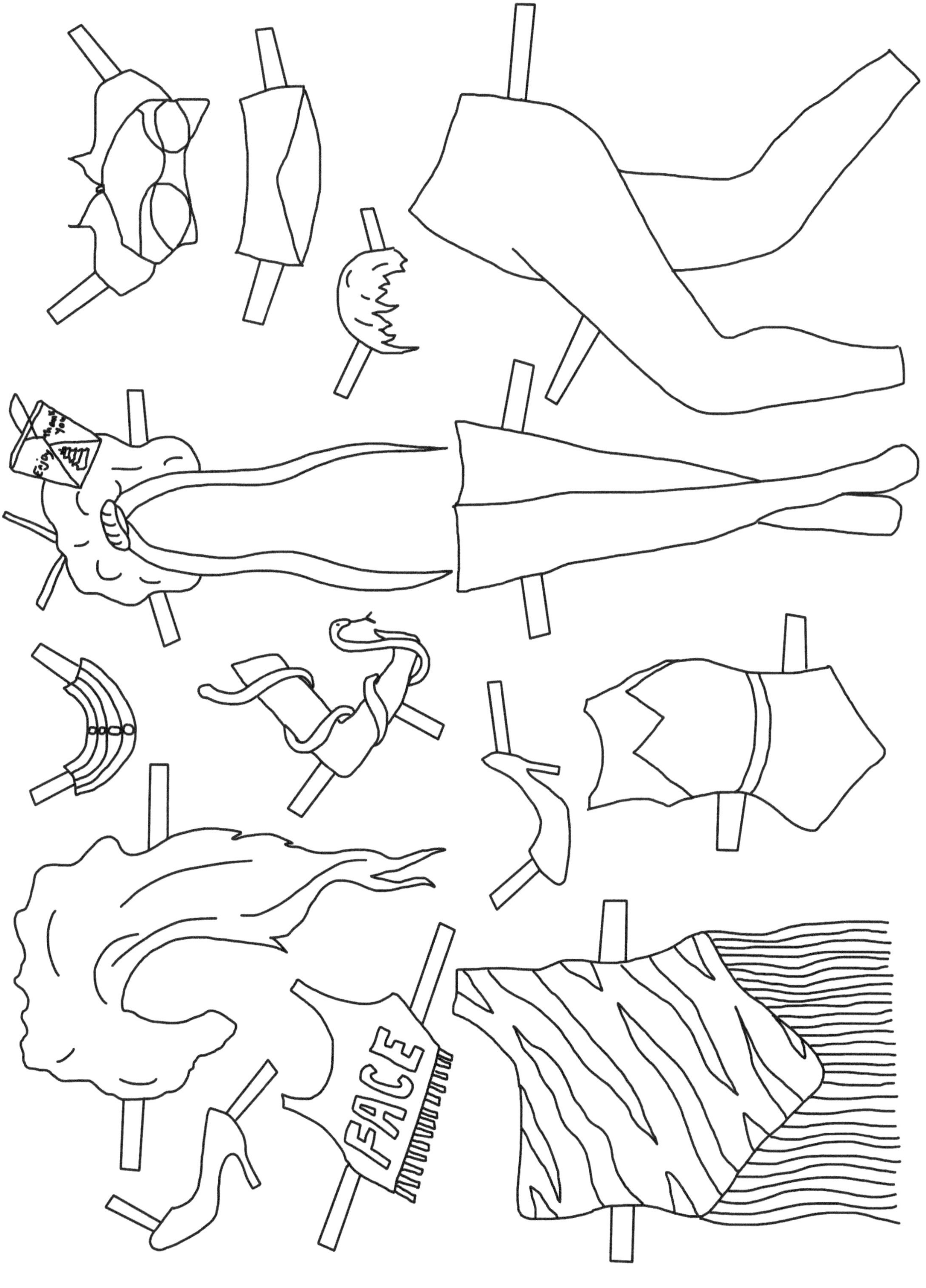
FACE

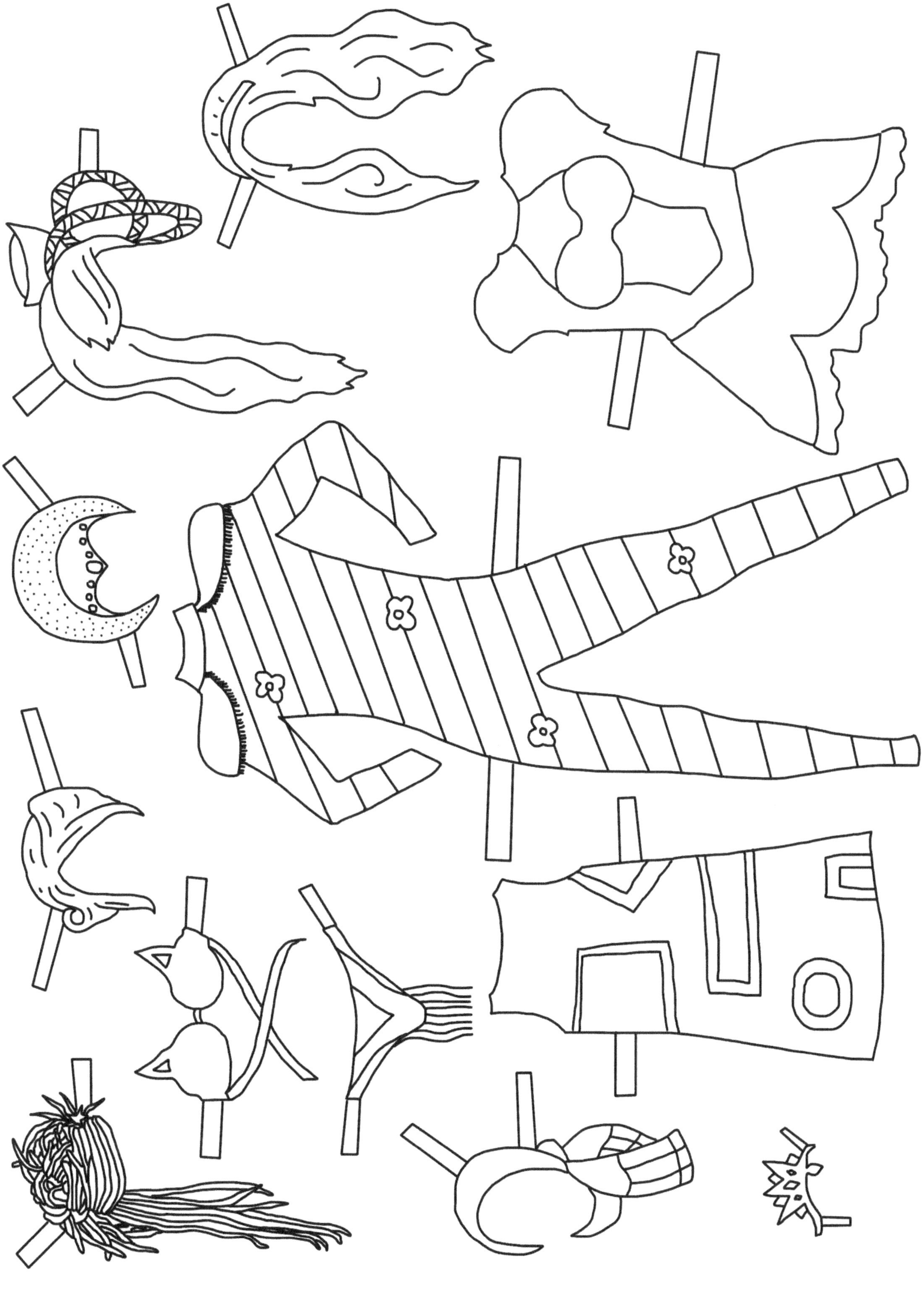

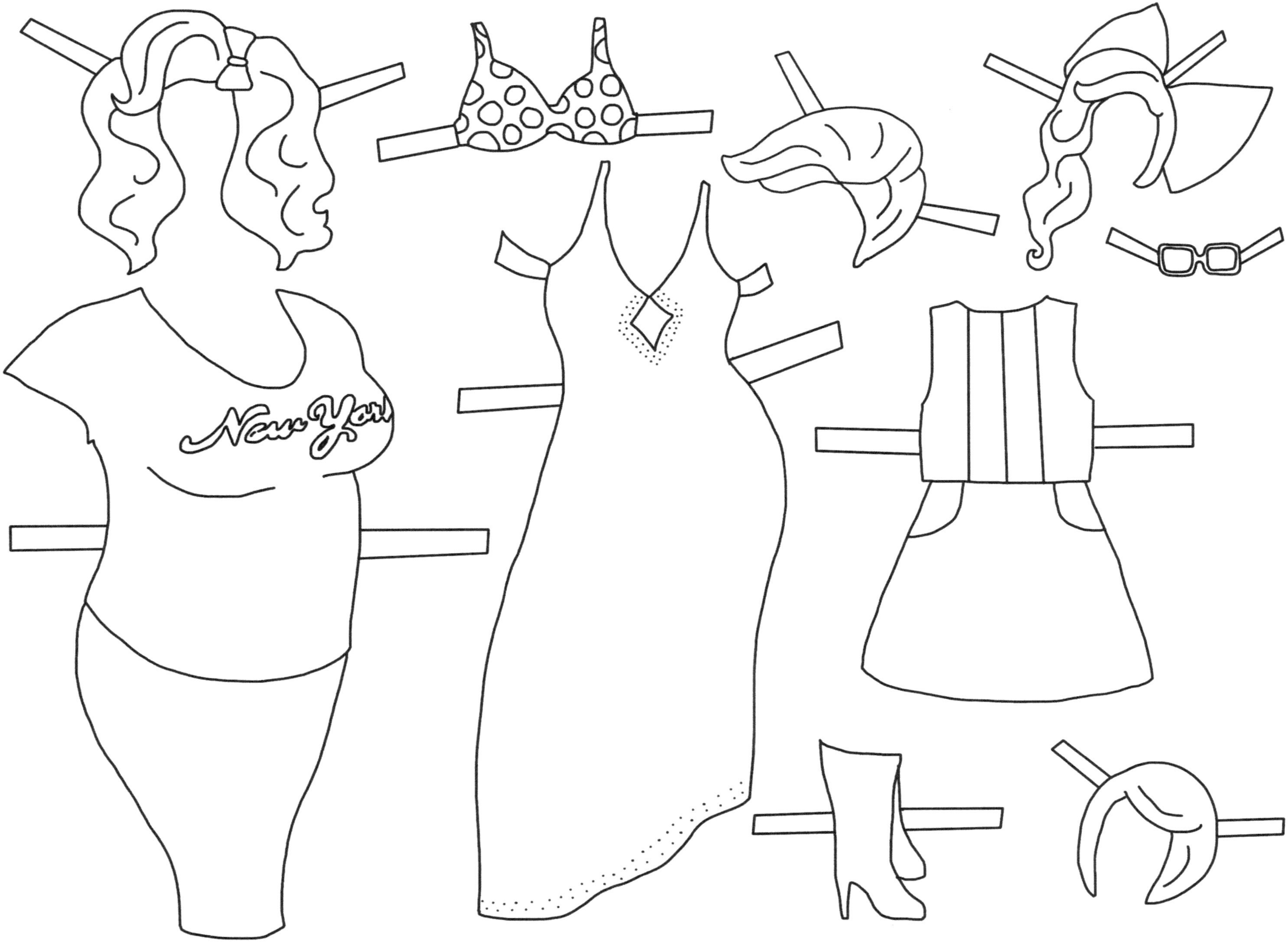
New York

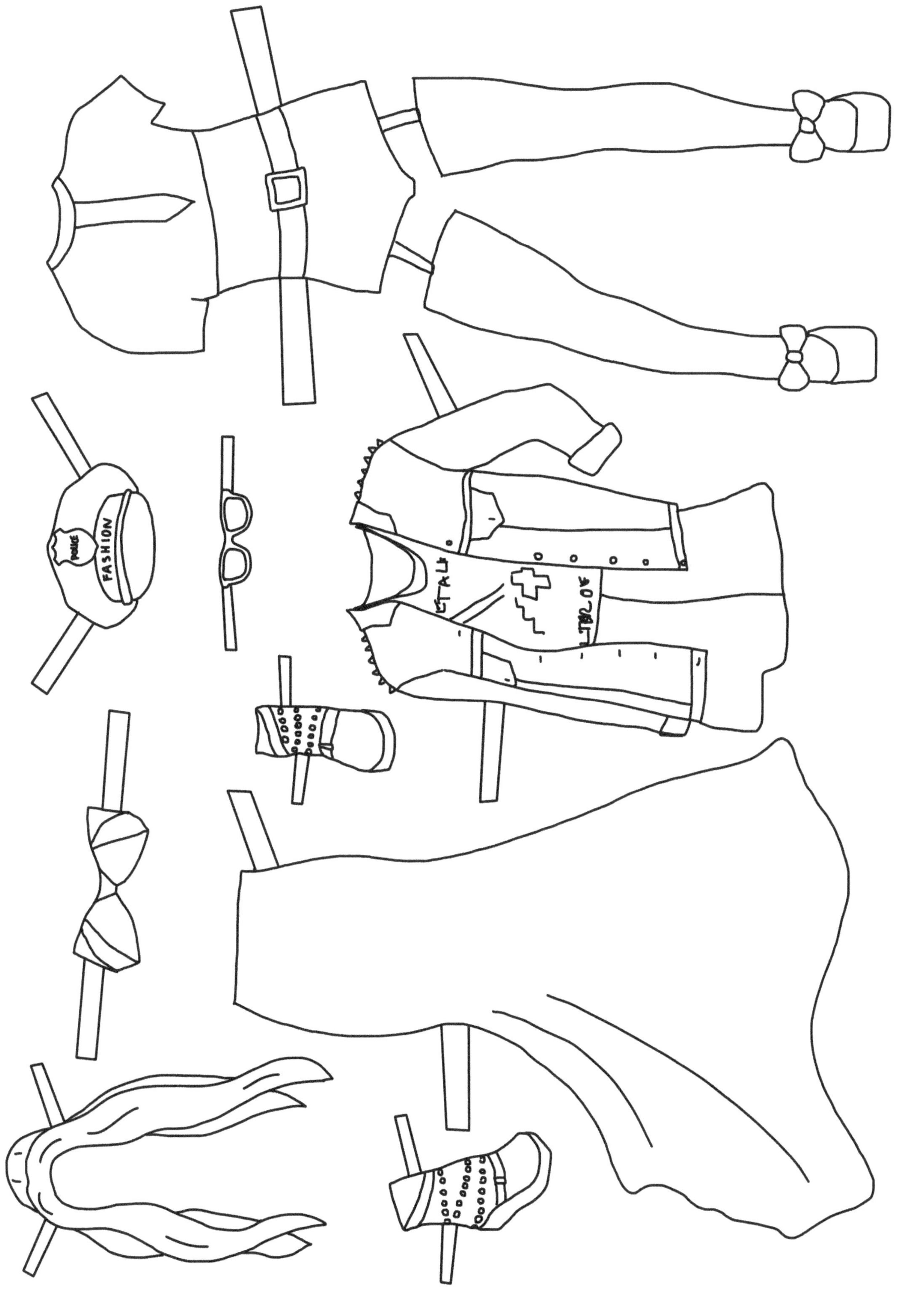
POLICE
FASHION

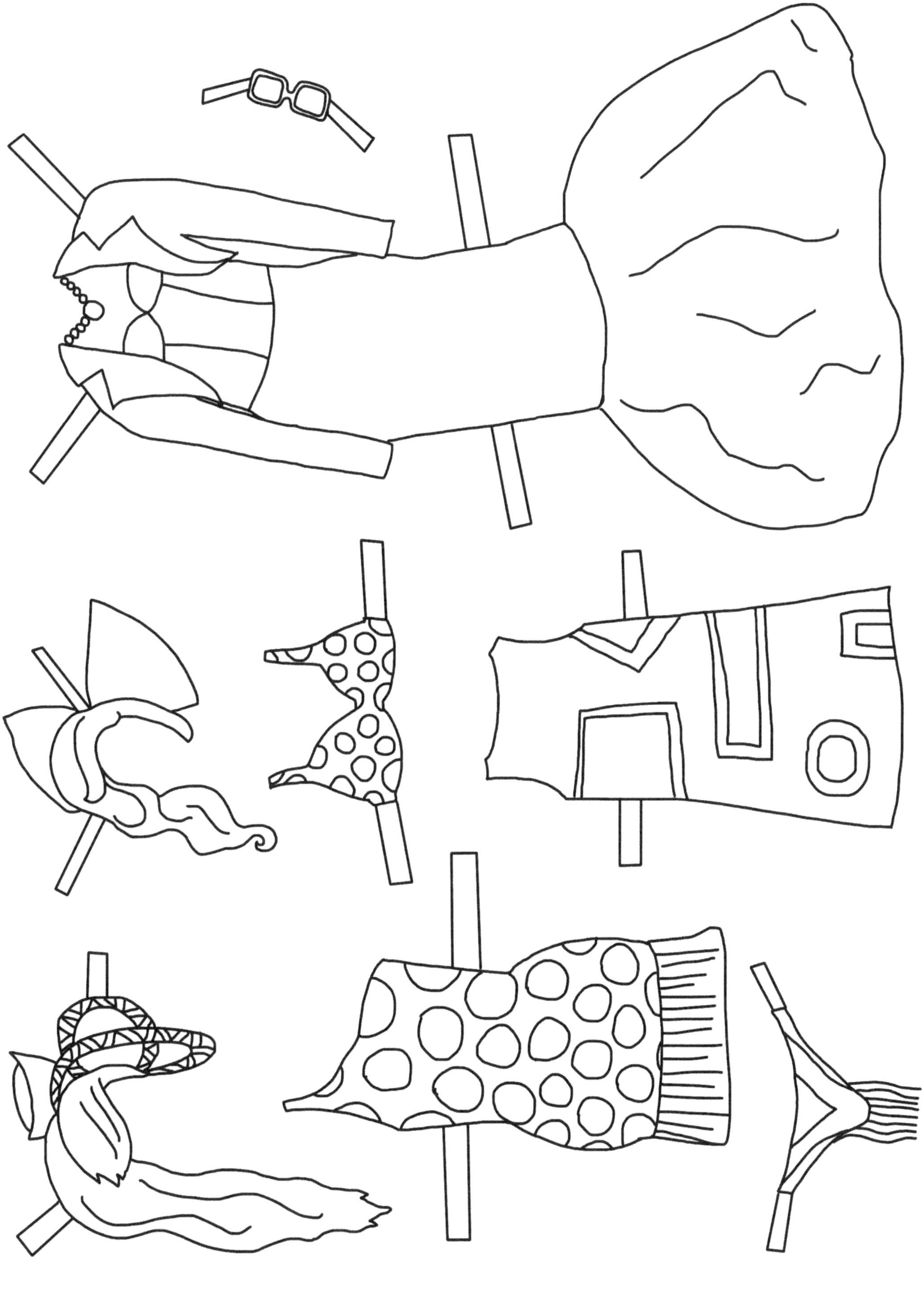

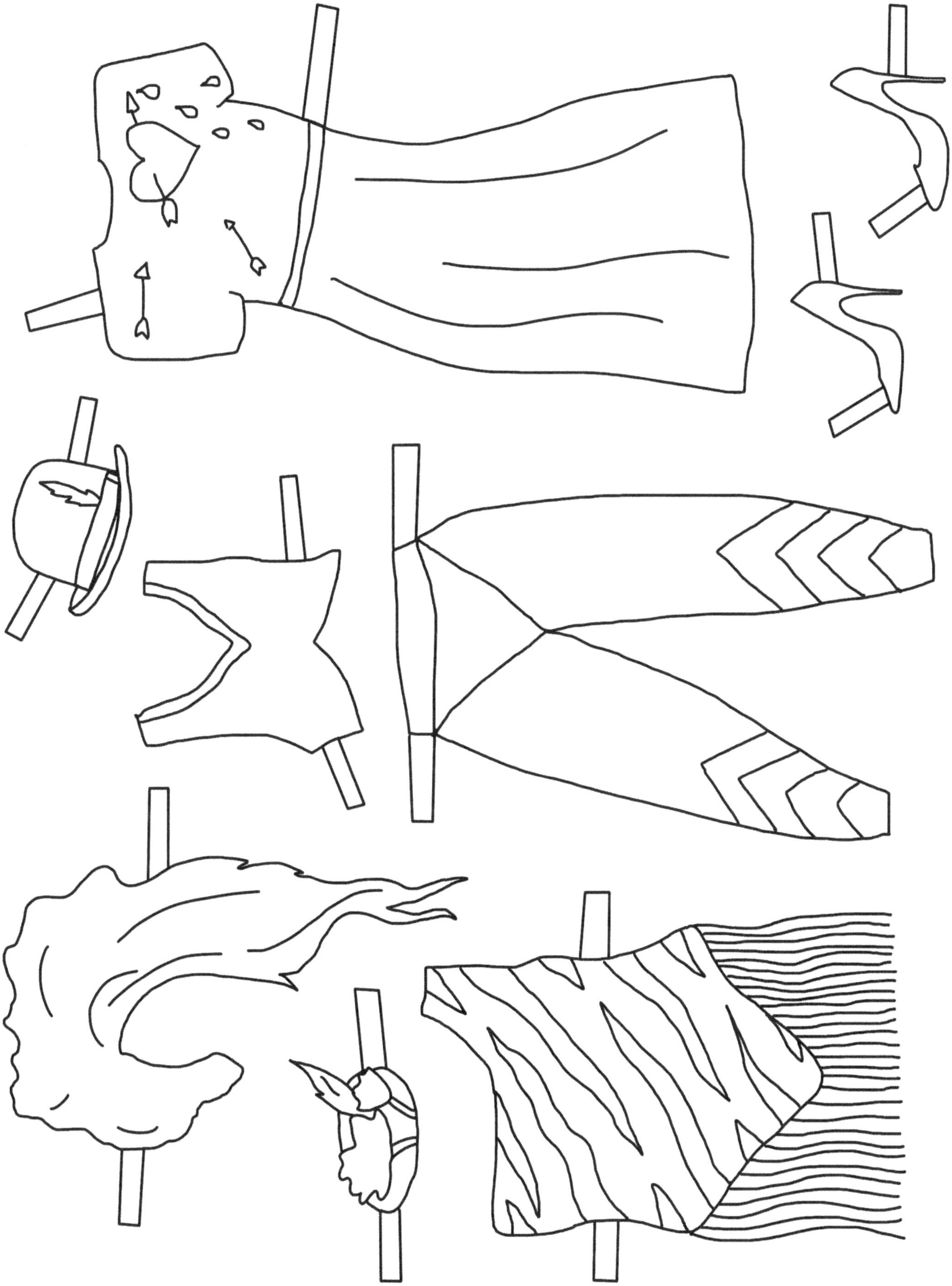

www.ingramcontent.com/pod-product-compliance
Lightning Source LLC
Chambersburg PA
CBHW081849170526
45167CB00007B/2949
* 9 7 8 1 5 4 2 9 0 2 8 5 4 *